Not So Bad

From The Bronx to Beverly Hills

Not So Bad!

Larry

Not So Bad

From The Bronx to Beverly Hills

By Lawrence N. Field

Introduction by Frank Gehry

Edited by Alexander Auerbach

Published by NSB Associates, Inc.

Cover design: Adams Kazeem

Cover image: The Wall Street Journal, used with permission

Back cover photo by Allison Cane

Published by NSB Associates, Inc.
433 N. Camden Drive
Suite 820
Beverly Hills, CA 90210

ISBN 978-1-7331455-0-3

www.NotSoBadBook.com

Dedication

In loving memory of Eris Madeline Perll Field, beloved wife, mother, grandmother and friend.

Introduction

My Friend, Larry Field

By Frank Gehry

Larry grew up poor. He started in business the first part of the early 1960's. I grew up poor and started my company in 1962. Neither one of us had any money when we started out on our own. He created a very successful real estate entity for himself.

I watched him go through the ups and downs of the market and his own trials and tribulations inside of his company. No matter what, Larry was always cool about it all. He was always playing the long game, investing in properties he believed in and people he believed in. He was always fair, but more than that, he was generous of spirit and generous of resources even when he didn't have to be.

I met Larry many years ago, sometime in the late '70s, early '80s. Freddy Weisman, an art collector friend of mine, was looking for a building to use for his collection. Larry was really sweet and helpful in his talking to us. We didn't really know what we were doing, but it didn't feel like he was taking advantage.

There was something about that deal that brought me back to him later. He had been so straightforward and easy to deal with that, when Chuck Arnoldi and I got the opportunity to buy the warehouse that we had been using for our studios, I called Larry. I said "How do you do this? How do you buy a piece of land? Can you give me a little crash course?" So, Larry, without personal interest, very generously gave me advice and mentored me through the process.

This was really extraordinary to me, because I did not know him well at that point.

Over that period of time, I got to know Larry pretty well. Berta and I went to his house for dinner, we met Eris and their kids. They came to our house, and it was really easy to become

Frank Gehry and Larry Field at Gehry Partners Studio
Los Angeles Times photo, used with permission

friends with him and his family. We didn't necessarily share the same ideas politically, but we certainly shared the same values. We also have the same kind of background, which means we really get each other.

About eighteen years ago, it got to a point where my office needed a larger space. We tried for six months to find something that would work, and we came up empty-handed. So I called

Larry and said, "Larry, please help me, I don't know what to do. We're desperate." Larry reassured me, saying, "Don't worry Frank, I'll figure it out, I'll take care of it for you." That's just the way he was.

Sure enough, a few hours later he called me back and told me he found a warehouse in Playa Vista, and a few hours after that, I found myself driving down with him, looking at this building. It was perfect, except it was twice the size that we needed, so Larry and I agreed to buy the property 50/50.

He was intriguing in his generosity and the way he talked, and that hasn't changed. He was just Larry, good ol' Larry then, and he is the same now. When you say "Hello Larry, how are things?" He says, "Not so bad!" That's his clarion call, and somehow over the years, it's become very reassuring, and it makes you feel at ease. The world is crazy, but we're okay. I found it very comforting then, and I still take comfort in Larry's "Not So Bad!"

The Very Expensive Diamond Necklace ... That Turned Out to be a Bargain

There are lots of reasons a man might have to buy his wife a very expensive diamond necklace. Notice I said "have to," not "want to." Usually it involves another woman, alcohol or some other kind of embarrassing behavior. In my case, it was a building.

For the more than 49 years I was lucky enough to have Eris as my wife, we had an understanding. I was very successful in business, especially real estate, so I was the one who was smarter about money. Eris was the one who pretended to believe that. In fact, of course, she was very astute, and I knew that. But I still got a costly reminder one evening in 1984.

A partner and I had built a large project in Los Angeles, which he was managing. Eventually I realized that he was taking money from the project that I thought should have gone to the partnership. I was really annoyed. The amount was too small to sue over, especially because half of it belonged to him anyway. But it was really difficult for me to be in business with somebody who would do that. I believe that if you can't trust someone about a small amount, you are foolish to think you can trust them on bigger ones.

I suggested to him that we sell the building. After thinking it over , he said he wanted me to buy him out. He said he thought the building was worth $10 million. The building had a big mortgage, maybe $8 million, so our equity was $2 million. I'd have to pay $1 million to buy his half interest. I really wanted to be out of the partnership, so I agreed.

This was December, around Christmas. I went home and told Eris. The building was owned by a corporation, which included my partner and me. As a formality, Eris had also been named as a director of the corporation, so she had to approve the transaction. I told her I was buying out my partner for $1 million.

She said, "A million dollars? I've been to that building. I don't like it. It's cheap, and I think the builders did a terrible job. I'll think about it, but I'm not going to sign it now." We then went out to a holiday dinner.

I was supposed to meet with him the next day, so when we got home I said, "Eris, what would I have to give you to sign this contract?" She thought about it for a few minutes, then said, "Well, "I'm really against this. I think you're overpaying terribly, and think you shouldn't do it."

"Okay. I understand all of that. But what can I do to get you to sign?". "Well, I always wanted to have a really lovely, antique diamond necklace. But it will be expensive."

I said, "Okay. Let's write it down." So we did: "I will buy you a diamond necklace at a price of no less $25,000 within 90 days of this date if you sign this agreement."

I signed it and gave it to her. She looked it over, said it was okay, and signed it. Then we went to bed.

I didn't get much sleep. I started thinking that she might be right, maybe the equity in the building was not worth $2 million, and I'm paying him $1 million for half the equity. I tossed and turned all night.

We were supposed to meet at my attorney's office at ten

o'clock. I got up about 6:30 a.m., and thought about it for another hour. Then I went to the bathroom, where we had a phone, called my attorney, Buddy Fischer, and said I would not be coming. I had changed my mind, and was not going to buy my partner's interest. I also told him about the deal I had made with Eris.

Then I called my partner, also from the bathroom so I wouldn't wake Eris, and told him a made-up story. I said, "I really am having problems with the bank where I'd be borrowing the money. They pretty much told me that they can't give me the whole million, they can maybe give me half. So we can't go through with it."

He kept me on the phone for 20 minutes, trying to change my mind. He offered to sign the deal now, and give me 90 days to raise the money. Then he said, "Just give me a hundred thousand now and owe me the rest."

He didn't just want to sell; he was desperate. Now I knew for sure that Eris was right, I'd definitely be overpaying. I told him I just couldn't do it, and hung up.

Eris and I on a snowy New York street in 1983

When I went back into the bedroom, Eris, who had been wide awake, said, "Who were you on the phone with?" "I wasn't on the phone," I said, which was pretty silly, because we had those multi-line phones where a button lit up when you were on a line. Eris could see from the phone in the bedroom that I had made two calls.

I said, "I was going to tell you at breakfast. I thought about it, and I think you might be right. What he wants to sell is probably not worth a million dollars."

I paused, then said, "So, since we're not buying it, you can give me back my note."

She said, "No, read the note. It says I get the necklace if I sign. It doesn't say that you had to buy him out, just if I sign. And I did."

Annoyed and only half joking, I said, "I'm going to call my attorney," who I had just talked to on the phone. I called Buddy again, let him know the deal with my partner was off, and about Eris' refusal to cancel the agreement.

"Let me talk to her," said Buddy. She got on the phone and he said, "Eris, you're absolutely right. Number one, he owes you the necklace. Number two, if you had called me first, you could have done much better."

I surrendered. I had been out-negotiated by Eris – not the first time, and not the last, but certainly the most expensive. I went to a jeweler and bought her a beautiful diamond necklace. Price tag: $28,000.

In October of the following year, my partner offered to sell me his interest in the building for $500,000. I said yes, and bought it. The end of the story is I sold the property some years later for a profit of about $2.5 million. It wasn't a great building, and the location wasn't very good, but the market was very strong at that time, making it a good time to sell.

So the very expensive necklace I bought for Eris actually saved me from overpaying by about half a million (well, $472,000 if you deduct the cost of the necklace), and enabled me to make a profit of almost 100 times what the necklace cost.

It was also a good reminder that, as smart as I thought I was about real estate, it always makes sense to listen to someone with an intelligent opinion. It's easy to become arrogant.

I guess I wasn't alone in that regard. Some years later I told this story at a luncheon where Eris was being honored by the Jewish Home For The Aging, where she was President of the Women's Auxiliary. There were about 500 people in the audience, and probably 460 of them were women. Every woman I met afterward said something along the lines of, "What a smart guy you were to listen to your wife. My husband doesn't listen to me even on small things, much less big ones."

They must have missed the part where I listened to Eris because an iron-clad contract forced me to.

At the time, I was in my mid-fifties, more than three decades older than the young man who left the Bronx to start his career, and an equal span of decades younger than I am as I write these words today. It's a good vantage point from which to look back at where I came from, and ahead to what became a very successful business.

Living in a nice Beverly Hills home in the 1980s, and arguing about whether or not to spend $1 million, much less in later years managing a portfolio of properties worth hundreds of millions, is quite a different life from what my parents, two Hungarian immigrants, would have expected for me.

My father ran a neighborhood grocery store in the Bronx. As an only child born in 1930, as the nation was plunging into the Great Depression, I was expected to help out in the store.

He started work at 6 a.m. or earlier, and didn't close the store until 8 or 9 p.m., six days a week and sometimes seven. My mother made salads at home for sale in the store, and candled eggs to spot flaws, but she usually didn't work behind the counter – which was just as well, since she had a rather difficult personality.

Compared to other families devastated by the Depression, we lived a relatively comfortable life, with not just the annual bungalow colony vacations but weekly dinners at Witkin's Deli. My parents had hopes of an even better future for me, as a school teacher or postal worker.

As it turned out, my life took a different direction from those honorable careers. I was very fortunate to have had the educational opportunities that the New York City public schools provided, and the free college degree that I received at what then was City College of New York, and is now Baruch College.

I was even lucky in the mistakes and happenstances along the way, as you will read in the pages that follow: training as an Army Ranger and getting lost by the Army; being so wildly successful selling soap that I couldn't get fired no matter how hard I tried; getting into real estate by accident when I was headed for training as a stockbroker; discovering what a tough steak can tell you about the value of a hotel; rescuing a frightened furrier hiding in his accountant's office; making sure the staff of the Japanese Pavilion of the 1964 World's Fair had someplace to live; and much more.

Of course, the most important lucky break of my life was getting invited to a weekend at Fire Island, where on a rainy July Saturday I met the beautiful Eris Madeline Perll, with whom I almost instantly fell in love. Fortunately for me, she felt the same way, and we were married just six months later. Our marriage lasted more than 49 years, ended in 2009 by the only thing that could part us, her passing to cancer. Together we raised two strong, independent daughters, Lisa and Robyn, and then saw our family grow with a wonderful son-in-law, Anthony, and two delightful granddaughters, Ibby and Kate.

This book, like this chapter, is a mashup of stories about my business career and my personal life, because they are inextricably entwined. Like all of us, what I've accomplished, or failed to, reflects who I am and where I came from.

I think it's worth telling, not because I happened to be successful in real estate – in that, I am far overshadowed by some of the titans in our industry, many of whom I know and consider good friends – but because my life is a demonstration that the American dream is a reality.

America allowed my parents, poor immigrants from Hungary who arrived in New York in the 1920s with no money, no connections, few skills and knowing not a word of English, to create a new life for themselves.

Working long hours through the depths of the Depression, they never became wealthy, or anything close to it. But they lifted me to the first rung of the ladder of success I was able to climb because of the opportunity that America offers to all.

Today's immigrants come from many additional lands, and speak other languages, and some who will climb that ladder are disadvantaged for reasons other than their birthplace. What matters about my story, and the countless others like it, is that it reminds us to continue to recognize the potential for success that exists in all of us, and to understand the benefits to society that we all enjoy when that potential turns into reality.

There are rewards that come with business success, of

course. Eris and I never cared for yachts or jets or extravagant mansions, but we had a very comfortable life. More importantly to us, we – and now I – have been able to assist worthy causes and organizations.

That's why I founded the Field Center for Entrepreneurship at Baruch College, which focuses on helping young people become entrepreneurs, and provides advice and support to business owners in the community.

It's why I funded the Field Medical Simulation Center at Ben-Gurion University of the Negev, which helps medical professionals hone their skills.

Another priceless gift I've been granted is getting to know a great many interesting and accomplished people, such as Ronald Reagan, Frank Gehry, Shimon Peres, Larry and Robert Tisch, Bill Zeckendorf, Chaim Potok, Zev Yaroslavsky and Gustavo Dudamel.

One gift I was not given was a perfect memory. This book is my recollections of events that shaped my life. But I am not arrogant enough to believe that I have accurately recalled those events, and the people, places and times associated with them, in precise detail.

To friends and colleagues who should be included in these pages, but who I have inadvertently omitted, and to those who spot factual errors in what I recount, I apologize in advance, and assure you that the only cause is faulty recall.

My Bronx Boyhood

I was born in the Bronx, in the West Bronx near the Washington Bridge (not to be confused with the George Washington Bridge.) Most of the families in our neighborhood had several kids, but I was an only child, so it was just me, my mother and father.

I don't remember much about our street, but I certainly remember the address: 1849 Andrews Avenue. If you look at it on Google Maps, the street and our apartment building are pretty much unchanged. Nearby were the Park Plaza Theater and the elementary school. There were no school buses back then; your mother walked you to school until you were big enough to go by yourself.

My grandmother, Esther Deutsch, lived there as well, with two of her unmarried daughters, Elise and Helen. Both girls had the benefit of going to American schools, while their older sisters, Elaine, Pepy and Selma, had immediately gone to work when they came over.

My father had come from Hungary in 1924. After the end of World War I, Hungary had a democratic government, which was soon overthrown by a communist group, which in turn was quickly toppled by army officers who imprisoned communists, Jews and leftists, killing 5,000 and imprisoning 75,000 more. In the early 1920s the country was in chaos, and much of its territory and 60% of its population was handed over to Romania, Yugoslavia, Czechoslovakia and Austria. On top of all that, he got a notice that he was being conscripted into the Army.

All of that gave him good reason to emigrate to America. There's also a story I haven't been able to confirm that he had borrowed some money from family members for a business venture that didn't work out, so maybe that gave him an additional reason to seek a fresh start.

He was lucky he left, as was his older brother Joseph, who had also emigrated and lived in the Bronx. Seven of their brothers and sisters stayed in Europe, and all of them perished in the Holocaust, along with more than 50 cousins.

When my father first arrived, he gave his name as Moishe, which is what the family called him even though his name formally was Moritz. On his immigration paperwork they probably put it down as close as they could get, which was Morris.

When he became a waiter, his boss told him, "You should be more American." A waiter and the maître d' of the restaurant decided that "Eugene" would be a good American name, even though his last name was a not-very-American-sounding "Schonfeld." So he became Eugene.

His relatives, and his nephews who survived the war and eventually came to the United States (and eventually to Los Angeles — small world) continued to call him Moishe, as he was known in Hungary.

He came from a city called Munkacs (pronounced "mun-katsch"), which at the time was in eastern Hungary, and is now part of the Ukraine. It was part of the Austro-Hungarian Empire. Munkacs was a city of about 20,000 people, about half of whom were Jewish. Few Jews were affluent; most worked in the fields or did manual labor, while others had small shops or were craftsmen.

My father's father, my grandfather, was an exception. He

was a builder. In Europe he was called an engineer, but he built buildings. The book "The Vanishing World," by the photographer Ronan Vishniak, has several pictures taken in Munkacs, and in one there's a building my grandfather built.

I often wonder whether it's by chance that a grandson born in the United States, who never met him, should make his life's work erecting and buying buildings. Certainly I had no idea what I was going to do when I was in high school, or even in college. Yet by chance — or maybe not — I ended up in real estate.

My mother, Rose, had five sisters; Helen, Elise, Elaine, Pepy and Selma. Pepy was married to the wealthy person in the family, Max Liebowitz, who made ties. They had two children: Jerry, who became a doctor, and Viola, who was married to a dentist. They were quite a bit older than I, and their children were probably closer to my generation than they were.

My mother's older sister, Selma, lived in Aliquippa, Pennsylvania, about

Gene Schonfeld

25 miles north of Pittsburgh. She had been living in the United States for probably 15 years before my mother came over in 1920. She had two children. I got to know her son, Jimmy, quite well. Because of the 400-mile distance between Aliquippa and

New York, we didn't get to see them very much. At that time it was a big trip to go to Brooklyn from the Bronx, let alone to Aliquippa, Pennsylvania.

That was my closest family. I don't remember my grandfather, my mother's father, at all. I have pictures of him with a beard, but that's about it. But I of course remember my grandmother Esther, who lived in the same apartment house. It was really very good having her there.

My father was a very outgoing, gregarious person. Working as a waiter, with his "American" name of Gene, suited him. He got to meet a lot of people, which he liked, and they tended to like him.

The 1920s was the era of mobsters like Al Capone, Lucky Luciano and Bugsy Siegel – whose brother many years later was my doctor and good friend – and of gamblers like Julius "Nicky" Arnstein, who married the actress Fanny Brice. Gambling was illegal, but it was widely available in private clubs in New York City.

The last place Gene worked, the Hotel Ansonia, also had gambling. (It is still there, at 72nd Street and Broadway.) He would bring home marble poker chips they used for the games. I'm sure that drove everyone crazy, because he would break a set to bring home these big, thick chips they used for playing poker, but which for me were toys.

Gene was probably around five foot six inches tall, maybe five seven— not fat, but heavyset. I look somewhat like him, but twenty pounds heavier. As he got older he lost weight, and his brownish hair turned to gray. He was fun-loving, and whenever he could he spent time playing with me. He taught me to play pinochle, gin, casino, and checkers. He was very interested in people and very easy to talk to. Everybody liked Gene.

In 1936, when I was six, my mother convinced my father – probably almost bludgeoned him – to stop working as a waiter, which she apparently felt was not a very classy job. He bought a grocery store from the family of one of my mother's cousins, the Kleins.

That pleased my mother, except for the fact that the store was at the other end of the Bronx, in a section of the East Bronx called Throggs Neck. That was about as far away from where we lived as you could get and still be in the Bronx. No subway went there. You had to take a trolley that ended at what is now Bruckner Boulevard, then walk to another trolley, take that to Westchester Square, and then get a train. So we moved to an apartment on Calhoun Avenue, a couple of blocks from the store.

My father and I (wearing two different shoes) at the beach in 1934

The grocery store my father owned was probably 15 or 16 feet wide by about 50 or 60 feet deep. It was a pretty diverse neighborhood, with Italians, Germans and a sprinkling of Jews.

On the corner next to my father's store was a drugstore. The pharmacist was Jewish, as were a lot of pharmacists at the time. On the other side of our store was a shoe repair place, run by an Italian. Next to that was a bar, whose owners were Irish. Then there was a barbershop, run by some German barbers.

So our neighborhood stores were the pharmacy, the shoe repair place and the barbershop, where I got my hair cut when I was a kid. The only place we didn't frequent was the bar, because my father didn't drink beer.

My father always wore a shirt and a tie in the store. At the time, everyone who worked in a grocery store, even the clerks, dressed like that. He'd wear an apron over his jacket, except on the hottest summer days. There was no air conditioning at that time. In the store he was as outgoing and gregarious as he had been when working as a waiter. His customers loved Gene the grocer.

Like my father, my mother was meticulous about how she looked, but she was completely opposite to him in her personality. She dressed nicely and dyed her hair, even though they really didn't have any dates and didn't go out with other people. She didn't have a close circle of friends.

She was fastidious about her appearance, and would go to the beauty shop to have her hair and nails done. She was always dressed up when she left the apartment. She would not think of wearing a housecoat outside our home.

She was very presentable to the outside world, but it was a mask for her to hide behind. She was reclusive, antisocial, somewhat depressed and almost fearful of people.

She was very sensitive, even with her sisters. She would frequently take offense at something they said, and not let it pass. As I got older, she would say and do things that would bother me. I would suggest that she go out and do things, but she didn't like the movies. Neither she nor my father read much, because neither really mastered English. So she really had no outside activity.

The only times I remember her being a little outgoing was when her mother and sisters came over, or we visited them. Then she would talk freely. She had a hard time making small talk or even being civil to people.

She may have been suffering from some sort of mental illness, such as agoraphobia, the fear of leaving the house. I never knew. It always bothered me that she had no one to talk to but my father and me. My father's defense was to tune her out. And most of the time I was out of the apartment, playing with other kids.

The only time I really liked being around my mother was when she baked. She was a wonderful baker, and a great cook, skills she had learned in Hungary as a girl. All my friends would come around when she baked. She made cakes and passed them out, or I took them to school.

I have a feeling that their marriage was not a very happy one. It was just one that stayed together because there wasn't enough money to go their separate ways. In those days, people would get a divorce only in extreme circumstances, like spousal abuse or adultery. Short of that you just didn't get a divorce, especially among Jews. Maybe my parents weren't suited for each other, but they still stayed with each other all their lives.

My father managed his own life. He'd play cards with friends when they lived in the Bronx. When my parents retired to Florida, he played cards there too. He also worked, as a box boy at the local Food Fair supermarket, into his early eighties, just to get out of the house and keep himself busy.

The three of us on a rare outing together

On one of my visits to Florida he told me that the manager wanted to promote him to assistant manager of the delicatessen counter. I said, "That's great. What'd you tell him?" He said, "Nah, I told him I didn't want to. I didn't want that responsibility anymore." He liked the simple job of packing groceries.

"I do very well boxing the goods, because the women come with these baskets and bags. I never get to push their carts to

15

the parking lot. Most of the women just say, 'That's all right, Gene.'" They all knew his name. "They give me a dollar *not* to push it out!"

He didn't need the money. I was doing well, and was supporting them. He took the job to get out of the house. He would brag about it, saying "Larry, all these men here are so jealous." When I asked why, he said, "They don't have a job."

For him, having a job, being productive, was wonderful. He would work in the mornings when the other box boys, high school kids, were at school. After four hours in the store, he'd come home and play cards with friends.

He only stopped working because one day his supervisor asked him how old he was, and almost fainted when Gene said he was 79. He probably was about 83, maybe a little older. The supervisor made the manager fire him, because of concerns about insurance.

My mother's social life was primarily with her sisters. Most of her immediate family had come to the United States, and were not as affected by the Holocaust, while my father's family mostly stayed in Europe and was devastated.

Although she was not an outgoing person, at least when she helped in the grocery store she was forced to talk to people. She made the coleslaw, potato salad and other deli items. My parents pickled cucumbers to make pickles. At that time butter came in tubs, and my father or mother would take a knife and cut a pound of butter for a customer, and put it on some wax paper.

They, and later I when I worked in the store, served up the salads, cold cuts or whatever deli items the customers wanted. Liverwurst was popular, because it was cheap, and back then it seemed like I ate liverwurst all the time. To this day I don't eat liverwurst – can't eat it, can't even think about it. But I can still candle eggs or slice cheese like a pro.

From 1936 on I went to elementary school near Fort Slocum. As I got into older classes, maybe from the third or fourth grade on, I found it very difficult to make friends at school. Since I was Jewish I didn't go to a church, and everybody who was Italian or Irish went to the Catholic church.

I was pretty regularly chased by Irish or Italian kids,

especially when I went to the synagogue to take bar mitzvah lessons. My father had a hell of a time getting me to go for those lessons, because with so few Jews in our neighborhood, none of the boys I knew were going.

Most of the time, though, I played with other kids without anybody thinking about Jew or Gentile, Italian, German, Irish, whatever. We had what was probably the biggest playground in the city, a huge expanse of undeveloped land right here in the Bronx. We called it the swamps. A catch basin for rainwater runoff, it was about 800 to 1,000 feet wide and extended a long, long distance. We would play hide and seek, ball games, you name it.

A couple of decades later, when they built The Cross Bronx Expressway, and then the Throgs Neck Bridge, they cut through what had been our playground.

Our neighborhood had people from a lot of different countries, practicing a lot of different religions, but it was pretty homogeneous

In front of our home in the Bronx, in 1937

financially. Nobody made a lot of money, including my father. I don't think he ever made more than $10,000 in any year.

I worked as a box boy by the time I was 11, at the start of World War II, putting customers' groceries into a carton or bag. If it was a big order – $6 would fill a large bag – I would put it in the big basket over the front wheel of our delivery bicycle and take it to the customer's apartment.

When I was 14 I began using our family car for deliveries. It wasn't legal for me to drive, but I was never bothered by the beat cops, who knew us and almost everyone else in the neighborhood. In high school, I ran the store for a week every summer, so my parents could take a little vacation in a motel-like "bungalow colony" outside the city.

I learned to deal with people, including grownups, early on, when I began delivering groceries for my father. I guess watching my father interact with customers showed me how to behave. He was very good at it, and everybody liked him. And he did it working a minimum of ten hours a day, six and seven days a week. That's heroic.

I guess I was 10 or 11 or so when I got involved with the police. Some friends of mine and I were fighting with another group of kids. We climbed up onto a garage, and began taking small asbestos tiles off the roof and flipping them through the air, toward the other kids. All of a sudden a cop shows up, makes us get down, and arrests three of us. Well, he didn't really arrest us, but we didn't know that. He took us to the police station, which was a few blocks away.

He made us sit and wait on a bench at the police station. Then he said, "You know what you did is very bad. You could go to jail." He gave us a stern talking-to. Then he turned to another cop and said, "What do you think, Mike, should we put 'em in jail?" Mike thought about it for what seem to us to be hours, then said, "Well, I don't know, this is their first offense."

That "close call" was frightening enough, but then they put us in a car and drove each of us to our homes, so our parents saw us being taken out of a police car. That, you can be sure, was followed by a stern parental lecture. But it taught me a lesson: be very, very careful of other people's property, and not to do anything that might seriously injure another person.

My other experience in law-breaking, and a lesson well-learned, involved comic books. There was a candy store on Tremont Avenue, the main commercial street in our neighborhood, where we would go to buy comic books and get a soda.

One summer, my friend began stealing comic books by putting one book into another, paying a nickel for one and getting two. So I did it – actually, I outdid him. I took four comics, and slipped them together to make two pairs. I bought two and stole two.

I got home and my mother says, "You have four books. I only gave you a dime. Why do you have four?" I'm a terrible liar, and I hate to lie. So I mumbled, "Well, I…" She said, "Well, how'd you get the four?" I confessed that I really paid only for two and I stole two.

She called my father. Our apartment was only a few blocks from the store, in a two-family house. My father came home and really lectured me on stealing. He said, "You should not take anything that doesn't belong to you. No matter what the value is, it's not yours and you can't do it. It's something that will change you if you continue to do that."

Then he says, "Now you have to go back to Mr. Birnbaum," the owner of the candy store, "and tell him that you stole these two books and you're sorry and you apologize, and give him the dime you owe."

Well, the lecture was bad enough, but making me go back to the person I stole from, to tell him

Ready for sixth grade

that I stole the comics and pay him the dime, was much worse. Mr. Birnbaum simply looked at me, then quietly thanked me, but the feeling of shame was something I never forgot.

To this day, if I'm in a coffee shop or someplace and they make a mistake on the bill and they don't charge me for something, I point it out to them. That's the effect it had on me, after all these years, an event over 80 years ago. It was a simpler time. There was no television. We would listen to *The Lone Ranger, I Love a Mystery, The Shadow,* and *The Green Hornet* on the radio. Those shows really made you use your imagination. Watching television, you don't have to visualize anything in your mind. On the radio, they would describe things. In *The Lone Ranger,* you had to picture the horse galloping down the road. In *The Green Hornet,* you just heard the noise of the car, and you imagined that the car looked like whatever you wanted. I think it made children use their imagination more.

We kids went to the movies on Saturdays. Your parents would give you a quarter. The movie ticket cost a dime, and sodas, popcorn and candy were each a nickel. With one ticket you could stay the whole day. Each showing had two movies, which they called "features," plus cartoons, newsreels and a serial.

The serial was like a movie cut up into ten sections of about 15 minutes each. They showed one episode every week, ending each with a cliffhanger so you'd come back the following week to see what happened next. Some of the popular serials were *Flash Gordon, The Lone Ranger, Captain Marvel, The Green Hornet* and many others.

Then they'd show cartoons, and Movietone News of the World, where you'd see new and interesting stuff from all around the country and the world. The news was a week late, or more, but no one cared. With all of that, and maybe sitting through a second showing, you could easily be there for five or six hours.

When I was a kid, my mother tried hard to get me to play the violin. We had a violin they had gotten somewhere, so I took some lessons. My mother played the violin when she was young, and her brother became a violinist. But I didn't inherit those skills. At the end of four months, the teacher said to my mother, "Well, Larry's never going to play the violin." Eventually the violin went to somebody else. I hope they did better with it than I did.

It wasn't just that I had no interest in playing the violin.

I didn't want to stay home, for that or anything else. I wanted to play stickball with the other kids, in the middle of the street. All you needed was some kids, a rubber ball, and a broom handle. There weren't many cars at the time, especially on residential side streets, so those streets were our ball fields.

Hits were measured from one manhole cover to another. A two-sewer hit was fabulous. Three sewers put a kid in the ranks of Joe DiMaggio or Babe Ruth.

I played with whoever was in the neighborhood. The games were very simple – marbles, hopscotch or bouncing a ball against the steps of the stoop. We played with chestnuts on a string, hitting a chestnut with a stick to see who could break it. You'd get five shots, and then it was the next kid's turn. We'd heat up the chestnut, make a hole. and tie the string through. One guy would hold the string, and you'd take a swing at the chestnut. That was it.

Unlike today, when kids' days are scheduled to the minute, there were no classes or organized activities. A gifted kid might take piano or violin lessons, but that was about it.

A lot of the kids would hang out in ethnic groups – the Italians, the Irish, and the Germans. We did mix for sports; if we had a pickup softball or baseball game, the teams were made up of whoever was around.

There was prejudice, and words like "kike" were used. Philip, a kid

With my parents, at about age 12

from a German family, called me a name and we got into a fight. I wound up on my back, with him on top of me. I brought my legs up around his neck and smashed them down, slamming his head on the sidewalk. He was unconscious, and for a horrible few minutes I thought he was dead. But he wasn't. We took him to the drugstore, where they patched him up, and he was okay. For quite a while, though, nobody bothered me, because everybody had heard what happened to Philip.

Most of the time we hung out with kids from school, but it got more cliquish as we got older. In elementary school, I played with everybody. In high school, I primarily hung out with a couple of close friends, but would play football and softball pickup games whenever I could. There were some groups I couldn't get into unless they needed me, so with them I was always picked last.

I remember that some guys would sometimes chase me as I walked to the synagogue for my bar mitzvah lessons, but I never felt that I had suffered terrible discrimination. I realized that the name-calling, things like "Christ killer" or "kike" or "yid," was only what they heard at home.

The shoe repairman in the shop next to our grocery used to call me "morta cristo," which I found out years later was Italian for "Christ-killer." Yet he would do anything for me or my family. It was just a kind of nickname. And I did the same thing. I would call a kid a "kraut" or "wop." It didn't have the same terrible, searing impact that it has today.

I was more concerned that I wasn't prepared for my bar mitzvah. I wasn't very interested, I skipped a lot of lessons, and didn't work very hard at the lessons I did go to. The long-suffering Hebrew teacher probably made only $10 a week. He stood with me on the bimah when I said the prayers and read from the Torah, and probably half the words I said came from his mouth. I was very bad at Hebrew, and he would whisper each word to me as I struggled through the readings. With his help, I did get through the bar mitzvah, and afterward we had a Kiddush, a small reception, in the synagogue.

That night at our house we had some of our family over. My mother and father had no friends in Throggs Neck, and none of our customers were invited, so the only people there were our family, probably 15 people. I got a pen, a $25 savings bond from a rich cousin, and some cash, plus some gifts mailed by relatives who couldn't come.

I put the money away. I didn't spend it on anything. Even then I didn't have a great desire for things. Oh, I might save up for something I wanted that was special, as I did for a pair of binoculars I really wanted. But "things" were never very important to me. That included clothing. I was a pretty stocky kid, and once a year my mother would take me to Barney's, which had clothes for boys who were heavy. Barney's later became known for luxury clothing, but back then it was the store for heavy kids.

Field's Grocery, on Tremont Avenue
New York City Municipal Archives photo

Around this time, in the late 1930s, the East Bronx was a decidedly working-class neighborhood. The only "wealthy" people were doctors, although that may have reflected the respect people had for them more than real affluence. People who owned real estate were regarded as being very rich, but they generally didn't live in the neighborhood. I sometimes think that the way we equated owning real estate with being wealthy may have subconsciously influenced my career decision years later.

All the families I knew lived in two-story, two-family houses with a shared driveway going to the back yard, where there was usually a garage and clotheslines. Housewives would wash clothes by hand and hang them on a line to dry, because there were no washers and dryers. Bendix sold the first home washing machine in 1937, and it was far too expensive for anyone in our neighborhood to even think about buying.

Few of the wives worked. My mother did, because we lived about three blocks from our store and she would make the salads. That was her main job. On rare occasions, she'd spend an hour or two in the store to relieve my father.

My father didn't experience prejudice in the store. Everybody really liked him, and people who didn't have money knew they could get credit at his store. At the supermarkets, which were primarily A&P (nobody ever called it The Great Atlantic & Pacific Tea Co.) there was no credit. The supermarket prices were a little lower than at our store, but you didn't get Gene's jokes along with your purchase.

My father's name went through an impressive series of changes. He was born Moritz Schonfeld, but was called Moishe in Hungary, then became "Morris" after he went through Ellis Island. When he worked as a waiter he was urged to adopt a more "American" first name, and was dubbed "Eugene." His last name, Schonfeld, survived all of these changes, but then it too was overhauled.

My father used to tell me he decided to call it "Field's Grocery" because its front was so narrow – about 15 feet – that he didn't have room for a sign saying "Schonfeld's." (Schonfeld is a derivation of "schoen feld," German for "pretty field.")

It's a cute story, but there never was a big sign saying "Field's" on the front of the store. A more likely reason for the name was the desire – common among immigrants at the time, especially as across the Atlantic war threatened to consume Europe yet again – to fit in and seem less "foreign." Gene's tale about the size of the sign likely was his way of shielding his young son just a little longer from the harsh realities of the world.

Because of the store's name, a lot of people – customers, suppliers, delivery people and others – thought Gene's last name was Field. Eddie Sands, my father's nephew and the son of his brother Hersch, was an accountant, and he kept the books for the store. He said it would be less confusing for everyone if my father became Gene Field instead of Gene Schonfeld. Eddie, of course, had changed his own last name, although how he got "Sands" from "Schonfeld" I have no idea.

Field Chas 1840GrndConc ....TR emnt 2-5129
Field Creston Corp 2320CrestnAv .FO rdhm 4-8872
Field David MD 1401GrndConc ...JE rome 7-5631
Field Edw 3444KnoxPl ....OL invl 5-1138
Field Electrcl Instrument Co
                2734JeromAv RA ymnd 9-4731
Field Eugene grocrs 3752 ETremAv TA lmadg 2-7167
Field Frances 1515SelwynAv .....TR emnt 2-1121
Field Frank 3560 OlinvilAv ....OL invl 2-2236
Field Frank A Mrs 1576LelndAv .TA lmadg 2-3038
Field Fred E 1325LafyetAv ......DA ytn 9-1716

Our store's listing in the 1940 Bronx phone book

It wasn't unusual back then for people with "foreign-sounding" names to change them to ones that were more "American." Issur Danielovitch Demsky became Kirk Douglas, Mladen Sekulovich took the name Karl Malden, Danny Thomas was born Muzyad Yakhoob, Vladimir Ivanovich Palahniuk became Jack Palance, Antonio Dominic Benedetto is the singer Tony Bennett, and Alphonso Joseph D'Abruzzo is better known as Alan Alda.

When I was in high school, one of my classmates dropped her very Italian name, as you will read in a few pages.

I remember my father was not particularly eager to make the change, but it turned out to be easier for him. I think I was in fourth grade when my name changed from Schonfeld to Field.

I took some hazing from other kids for a while, but before long it was as if I never had another name.

That often happens in life; something you consider so gigantic in your life barely gets remembered or even noticed by other people. In a month, it fades from the minds of most people, and after three months you have to remind people that it happened. We are all so concerned about what other people think about us, when the truth is, by and large people don't think about us much at all. It's human nature; they have a lot of other things on their minds.

I'll give you another example. I had a beard for 18 years, then one day I shaved it off. I don't think more than one out of three or four people even noticed enough to say, "Didn't you have a beard?" So, when something terrible or embarrassing happens, I just tell myself, "It will pass." After a while, it does. You may never forget it, but the rest of the world does.

In any event, my name became Field, to everyone else and to myself.

Delivering groceries for our store, I got to know different people and how they lived. It was a real education for a boy like me. When I was about 15, one of our customers was Mrs. Murphy, who was usually drunk or tipsy on the afternoons I brought in her groceries. She would sometimes say, "Do you want to have a drink, Larry?" And I'd say, "No, no, I don't drink." I knew her kids. They were already out of high school, and working.

I always knew I had to be careful around Mrs. Murphy, because I had the feeling that if I wanted to, she would have entertained me in ways my parents would not have liked.

I would put down her groceries, stay far away, and get a quarter. If I stayed longer and talked to her, I'd get half a dollar. She was about 40, and she had two or three grown children, so she must have been a young girl when she got married. Her husband was a plumber. God knows what her life was like at home with him, that caused her to drink like that. Of course, I never thought about that at the time.

Another person I would deliver to regularly, Mrs. Simpson, was younger, and must have had eight or nine children. There were always three or four little kids around, some of them in diapers, and she'd be screaming and hollering at them. Sometimes I would get a nickel from her, and sometimes nothing. My father would tell me I had to collect the last month's bill from her. She'd look in jars and pots all over the kitchen, to scrape together some money to reduce her bill.

I don't know what her husband did, but whatever he did it wasn't enough, because they were always scraping bottom.

There were no high-rises in that part of the Bronx. Most people lived in two-family houses, although a few very large families lived in one-family houses. Rent was $20 to $30 a month for a two- or three-bedroom apartment.

Wages were low. I'd say the majority of our customers made maybe $25 or $30 a week. Some worked for the city, or the bus system, others were plumbers or electricians, some worked in warehouses and factories, some were truck drivers, and some worked in offices.

A big grocery order would be $6 to $8; a $10 order was gigantic. Cheese cost 15 cents a pound, butter about the same. A can of beans was eight cents, and most canned goods were anywhere from six or eight cents to 12 cents. Coffee was expensive: 20 cents a pound. A quart of milk was 15 cents. Eggs were 15 cents a dozen. A loaf of bread was a nickel. Ivory soap was three or four cents, while a fancy brand like Lux was a nickel.

We candled the eggs that we sold in our store. Candling eggs meant putting them over a metal box with a bulb inside it, and a hole just large enough to put in part of the egg. You would look at the egg and, with the bulb behind it, you could see through the shell. To me it was like magic. You could actually see the yolk and the white part inside the egg.

If you saw a streak of red in the egg, that was blood, and we would put that egg aside. No customers wanted to make scrambled, fried or poached eggs with bloody streaks in them. We sold them for a nickel a pound to a bakery a few blocks from the store. It didn't matter to them, it got lost in the cooking process.

I learned to drive from a Swedish man named Hannes Swenson who worked in my dad's store as a clerk. He was in his twenties. He taught me to drive because my father's driving ability was questionable at best. I started learning to drive just before my bar mitzvah, and at 14, thanks to Hannes, I started driving the car to deliver orders for the store.

At that time, you could get a junior license at 14, which meant you were supposed to have an adult with you when you drove. At 15 you got a full license. I did get a junior license at 14, but I drove by myself.

The cops didn't care. They'd see me driving, and knew how old I was. But the police at that time were really part of the community. They knew my father, Gene, they knew Field's Grocery, and the drugstore and the candy store and the bar. They walked their beat. Nobody feared them. We respected them, because we knew them.

On Sundays my father closed the store at five o'clock instead of staying open until eight, so we could have a family dinner. At first we went to Witkin's Delicatessen on 180th Street. That was our Sunday outing. Later, my parents wanted to go to a fancier place, so we switched to the Bruckner Diner, on Bruckner Boulevard. The next step up was a Howard Johnson.

As I got older, I began to notice that my folks would always have a hamburger steak. Wherever they went, they always had the same thing. I asked why. "We know what it is. We like it." That was always their answer.

Later I realized they had the hamburger steak because my mother and father had very poor teeth. My father had a full set of false teeth. My mother didn't have a full set, but had some. So it was safer to have a hamburger steak than anything hard to chew.

The 1939-1940 World's Fair was big news when I nine years old, but I was taken there only once or twice. It covered 1,200 acres of Flushing Meadows Park, which was also the location of the 1964-1965 World's Fair. There were pavilions from all over the world – England, France, Greece, Japan, the USSR, even a Jewish Pavilion a decade before the establishment of Israel. It was like a fantasyland just walking around the place.

They called it "The World of Tomorrow," and it was. I remember the General Electric exhibit. At home, like most people in the Bronx, we had an icebox. I think the refrigerator came around 1941. At the World's Fair, GE had toasters, refrigerators, washing machines and dryers, even a television. These were all new to us and to almost every other visitor to the fair.

I remember they had a different kind of stove, the Radar Range, which was the forerunner of the microwaves. General Motors had futuristic cars, with body styling that didn't come out until the 1950s and `60s. IBM showed the forerunner of the computer.

Back then there were few ways to see these new things. They weren't in the movies, and TV had not yet arrived. But 44 million people got to see them at the fair.

Kids in my neighborhood also got a peek into the wider world because the Coast Guard Academy was in Throgs Neck, near us. People from all over the country attended the academy. We got to meet some of them, because for a four-year period the daughter of the academy's commandant was in our class. She would take us to play on the grounds, and into the mess hall.

We met her father, who was very different from the other adults we knew, who were mostly plumbers, electricians, carpenters, shopkeepers and truck drivers. She was also different from us kids because she had lived in a lot of places as her father was transferred from one post to another.

The 1939 New York World's Fair, celebrated on a 3-cent stamp.
Image courtesy Vintage Postage

I think meeting her father planted the idea in my mind of going into the military, but that was a decision that was years in the future. First I had to put in my hours at school and at the grocery store.

High School Days

I attended Christopher Columbus High School, on Pelham Parkway. My main high school memories involve the drama department, the swimming team, typing and the senior prom I never went to. I joined the drama department, but didn't get to perform much. I was pretty much a spear carrier. I didn't have any speaking parts. I just stood or walked around in the background.

We did have some talented kids. A very pretty girl, Anna Maria Louisa Italiano, was in a lot of plays. She later became the famous actress Anne Bancroft. One of the neighborhood kids, then known as Owen McNulty, later went on the stage as the singer and comedian Dennis Day, and eventually went on the radio and TV with Jack Benny. Another very good actor, and a good high school friend of mine, was Richie Davalos, who also went to Hollywood.

I took typing, because I thought it might be useful. I think there was only one other guy in the class, because boys didn't take classes like typing or home economics. It turned out that learning to type was an excellent decision, because I could type up my notes in college and law school, which was really helpful.

I joined the swimming team because I liked the sport, and got a half a credit for it. Swimming taught me to work as part of a team. Whether it's the relays or individual events, the team's score depended on whether you came in first, second or third. The team that got the most points would win, and of course we all wanted our team to win.

There was a lot of prejudice at that time. The German Bund had been active in Throggs Neck in the years leading up to World War II. I got into some scrapes with some of the German kids who had been told at home that Germany was right and Jews were bad.

It didn't affect me a great deal, because I usually went home as soon as the high school day was over, for two reasons. First, I didn't know a lot of the kids there, because I lived a streetcar and subway ride away. More important, I was now the main helper for my father.

During the war and afterward, it was very hard to get help. Hannes, who had worked for him (and had taught me to drive) went into the Army in 1942. My father couldn't replace him, because during the war everybody was working. There were plenty of jobs for any man not in uniform, and women went to work in factories, which was a huge change.

As the main helper for my father, I worked in the store after school until six or seven o'clock at night. The store was open from six a.m. to eight or nine at night. Some years later my father began to close at seven, the earliest he ever closed.

When I was in elementary school, my mother and I would go away to Rockaway for a couple of weeks during the summer. We'd have one little room in a little motel — something like a Motel 6 — with a hot plate. Some of my mother's sisters would come with their families. My father had to run the store during the week, so he would come and visit on a Sunday.

Later, when I was old enough, I would run the store for a week during the summer, so he could stay with my mother and our relatives. I did it during my junior and senior years of high school, and the first three years of college.

It was a very important experience, one of the milestones of my life. I didn't know what I wanted to do for a career, but after running the store for a week I decided that I would never, ever run a retail store. It felt like prison. You couldn't leave; you had to be there all the time.

Looking back, it's hard for me to imagine how shy I was. Today I can talk to anybody and ask anybody almost anything. But in high school I was the opposite, and that included being very unsure with girls.

Nevertheless, I thought I should go to the senior prom, so I picked out a girl who I sort of knew, and I thought was a fairly safe choice. Her father had a newspaper stand in a nearby subway station, so I wasn't intimidated by her the way I might have been by some girl whose father was, say, a doctor or an attorney or an accountant. Still, it took me weeks to get up the nerve to ask her.

She said, "Well, Larry, we really don't know each other, except saying hello in class. So, maybe, how about going out?" I hadn't thought of that. This was about six weeks before the prom, so we went to a movie and had coffee and a malt. That may have cost a dollar. Movies were a quarter, coffee was a nickel, her malt was ten cents. Then I took her home and said, "Well, what do you think?"

She said, "Well, maybe we should go

The (High School) Graduate, 1948

out one more time." It took me another ten days to go out with her again. Now the prom was about four weeks away. Again I asked her what she thought. She said, "You know, Larry, you're

33

a nice guy, a fine person. But I don't think I would want to go to something as special as the prom with somebody unless I really had some feeling for him." Clearly, that wasn't me.

Rather than feeling rejected, I realized I felt the same way, but wouldn't have had the courage to tell her. I thought it was wonderful of her to say, "I don't think it's good for us to do this. It would be fine, but it won't mean anything." So I never did go to my high school senior prom. But looking back, I am still amazed at how insightful she was.

Baruch College

I enrolled in the business school of City College of New York, or CCNY, in September of 1948. (In 1963, the school was renamed Baruch College, in honor of Bernard Baruch.) It was in Lower Manhattan, on 23rd Street and Lexington Avenue.

My time at Baruch was a critically important turning point in my life. My main reason for going there was that it was absolutely free, except for a $100 fee for registration and student activities. My folks couldn't afford to send me to go to a private college, because tuition, room and board would probably have been $5,000 to $7,000 a year, and my father was not making much more than that.

In my freshman year I joined a house plan, or group. They were named for graduation years, and ours was Ketchum '52. Why Ketchum? I never asked, and still don't know.

Ketchum '52 was a small group, 15 people, and we became – and stayed – close friends. We continued to get together pretty regularly for the next 60 years, usually in New York, because just about all of them lived there. One year, I put together a trip to California's wine country, and seven of the guys came with their wives.

When you get into your sixties, seventies and eighties, there are just not as many opportunities to get to know people as when you were in college.

Few of the Ketchum guys came from wealthy backgrounds. An exception was Irwin Horowitz, whose father had the Ethan Allen chain of furniture stores. Herb Dallis' father had a very successful coffee roasting company, which will become part of this story later. Al Bronstein came from a very modest family; I later went into real estate with him, and his brother-in-law probably helped save my wife's life.

Another guy, Bob Suttner, was an intellectual who became very wealthy almost by accident. He was going to be an economist, and went to England to study at the London School of Economics.

There he met Bernie Cornfeld, who with a few hundred bucks had started Investors Overseas Services, selling mutual funds to American soldiers stationed in Europe. Bob joined IOS, and made so much money that he never went back to school. This was way before any of the rest of us made much money.

Sheldon Itzkoff's story is also unusual. He had a hearing problem from a very young age, and hearing aids were only partially helpful. He went into human resources, and wound up as a vice president of the global accounting firm Deloitte & Touche.

As was common at the time, he changed his last name to Williams, which sounded more American WASPy. After he retired he changed it back to Itzkoff.

Elliott Lowell became a restaurant critic. Dave Oser, one of my closest friends, worked in the Catskills with me. Dave went into insurance, but switched to teaching adults in high school, at which he was wonderful.

So we had a group of smart, interesting guys, all of whom made great successes for themselves in their own ways. I'm very proud of that group of friends.

I also joined a Jewish fraternity, Sigma Beta Phi. Fraternities weren't big at Baruch. There were a few, but it wasn't like at private schools, where fraternity life was often very important.

Ours was not a national fraternity. There were just chapters at four or five schools in the New York area. We had a frat house, which was really a loft on 17th Street, about six blocks from the college.

The fraternity was a great way to make friends with other guys. The loft was handy if we wanted someplace private to be with a girl, but sex happened less than you'd think. Taking a girl to a hotel room was out of the question because of the cost, and all the guys lived with their parents. One or two hookers came to the fraternity house; the charge was five dollars, which few of us could afford.

Some of the guys in the fraternity went on to be very well known.

Mort Gerberg is a wonderful cartoonist whose work has appeared in *The New Yorker*, *Playboy*, in comic strips and on TV, as well as in his 43 books. I'm proud to have several of his original drawings.

Marvin Kitman was with Newsday for 35 years, wrote nine books, was a famous TV critic and humorist; he staged a mock run for president in 1964, and held a $1-per-plate fundraiser at an Automat in New York.

Carl Spielvogel started out as a reporter for the New York Times, then became a big name in advertising, auto dealerships and investing, and was made an ambassador by Bill Clinton.

Ralph Ginzburg became famous for creating *Eros* Magazine, a quarterly filled with classy erotica and serious articles. Ginzburg was arrested and convicted for indecency, released after a few months, and went on to start other well-regarded publications and write several books. *Eros* was scandalous back then, but today it would never sell; it would be too innocent.

Because I earned money working during the summers, I didn't have to hold a job while I was at school. I was able to join the drama club, called Theatron. I was on the student council, and I joined the staff of the student newspaper, the *Ticker*.

I met Ginzburg when I joined the *Ticker* staff. I was a freshman, and Ginzburg, a junior, was the editor. We called him "Windy," because of his long-winded discussions and his long articles. I eventually was appointed the features editor and wrote a column à *la* Walter Winchell.

We *Ticker* staffers acted like we were real newspapermen. We'd go to the printer one night each week to read galley proofs and check the copies as they came off the press. The paper was printed with metal type.

It wasn't like on today's computers, where you can revise anything in a moment. If you wanted to change something on a page, you'd have to pull out a line or two of type, then put in new words that if at all possible would have the same length, because otherwise it would change the way the column of type or even the entire page was put together. A change was a big deal, especially at two or three in the morning.

But "putting the paper to bed," as the press run was called, was exciting because we were doing something very different from sitting in a class. What we did at the *Ticker* was not much different than what real newspapermen did, except that we didn't get paid, and our paper only came out once a week.

There were two big news stories at the time.

One was the trial of Julius and Ethel Rosenberg, who were accused of stealing the secrets of America's atomic bomb program and giving them to the Russians. In college, everybody took sides, with some believing that they were innocent, while others were convinced they were dangerous spies who deserved everything the government could throw at them. They were convicted, and both were executed in 1953. After the Soviet Union fell, secret Russian documents showed both had in fact been spies. Whether they deserved to be executed is another story.

The other big story was point shaving by college basketball players. This was a form of cheating where players conspired with gamblers to deliberately miss some baskets in order to keep a game's score within the point spread the gamblers wanted. That was the bigger story for us, because some of the players involved were from City College.

During the school year, after girls, our other big interest was sports. The New York Yankees were my favorite, probably because they were in the Bronx. A friend of mine who lived in Brooklyn cheered for the Dodgers. There wasn't much football at all. Basketball was only played in gyms. There was no NBA to speak of. The Harlem Globetrotters were the big thing. We didn't play or follow golf. We'd follow tennis, which I played. I remember Pancho Segura and Pancho Gonzales. They were about my age. Years later, Gonzales taught at the Beverly Hills Hotel.

I went to very few baseball games when I was young. My father was too busy running the store to go to games. My mother didn't even go to movies, let alone a baseball game; she didn't even know what the game was about. When I was in high school, I would go to Yankee Stadium once in a blue moon. A few of us would take the bus. In college, I mainly went to basketball games to cheer for the CCNY team.

One of the most important parts of my education didn't take place at Baruch College. It was the Dale Carnegie course in public speaking, which I took because my friend Dave Oser had signed up and didn't want to go by himself.

It turned out to be a very valuable experience, because it helped me become comfortable talking with individuals and groups. I was just a college kid, and there were some very important people in my Carnegie class: the chief financial officer of Mobil Oil, a senior executive at Proctor & Gamble, and others. I remember being surprised that these successful businessmen were uncomfortable talking to groups.

At the end of the eight-week class, the instructor asked me to stay on for the next class as an assistant instructor. Then, for the class after that, I was made a Dale Carnegie instructor. It really helped me feel comfortable while speaking before a large group.

Talking to 20 or 30 people is very different from speaking one-on-one. You have to plan what you're going to say, and to get your point across you have to say it at least three times, in different ways. You can open with it, say something about it in the middle, and then finish with another reference to what you want your audience to remember.

I learned very valuable skills that have benefitted me for my entire career, just because I wanted to help a good friend who didn't want to go to the class alone.

When I was an instructor, some of the people in my class were vice presidents of big companies and other very successful people. I was a 20-year-old college student, and I was teaching them! I always told the people in my class that I was in college, and that if I could speak well at my age, so could they, once they got over their fear of public speaking. They saw that I knew what I was doing, and accepted me as their teacher even though I was much younger and far less experienced in the business world than they were.

That was an important lesson. If I knew what I was talking about and projected confidence, others would accept my leadership. So, while I helped the people in the class, in that way I think they helped me more.

1948 to '52 was a relatively quiet time in the United States. Harry Truman had become president in 1945, after the death of Franklin Roosevelt, and won reelection in 1948. Almost immediately after FDR died, Truman had to make the decision to drop atomic bombs on Hiroshima and Nagasaki, forcing Japan to surrender. Then he implemented the Marshall Plan to rebuild Western Europe, helped found the United Nations, oversaw the Berlin Airlift of 1948, and pushed for the establishment of NATO. In my view, Truman was one of the best presidents America has had.

He was succeeded by Dwight David Eisenhower, or "Ike," in 1952, just as I was finishing school. The United States was growing rapidly after the war, with new buildings going up, new jobs being created, new companies being formed.

The Catskills: My First Taste of Freedom

I started at Baruch in September of 1948, and the following summer, after my freshman year, I worked as a camp counselor. I made maybe $400 total. A year later, in the summer of 1950, I went to work in the Catskills, at the suggestion of a friend who had worked there the year before.

The Catskill Mountains, about 70 miles northwest of New York City, had blossomed as a resort area. Before the war, what was known as the Borscht Belt had a lot of low-end resort hotels, along with a few classy places like Grossinger's, the Concord and others. With the postwar surge in young families and incomes, many new resorts opened, and many of the older ones were fixed up.

I got a job at the Kiamesha Lodge in Kiamesha Lake. It was a middle-class hotel, not a fancy place, with 500 to 700 people there for the summer. The husbands would come up on weekends, while the wives and kids would be there during the week. There were not many singles at the Kiamesha.

I started out as a busboy, but after two weeks one of the

waiters got sick and had to leave, and I was chosen to become a waiter. I made a lot of money, because I was very good. In the Catskills, being a good waiter meant bringing vast amounts of food, and delivering it quickly. That was the whole trick. What most guests were interested in was three huge meals a day.

After dinner I got a short break, and at nine o'clock I'd start working in the snack bar. The hotel provided entertainment – singers, comedians, dancers and so on – in the early evening. Then the guests would come to the snack bar. Remember, those guests had started the day with a breakfast of eggs, lox, cereal, herring, cheese, vegetables, pancakes – you name it. Then they would have had an equally generous lunch, and an even more lavish dinner. And they were still hungry when they showed up at the snack bar!

I had two tables of ten in the dining room, so I was serving 20 people. We waiters got about $100 a week per table in tips. I was there for eight weeks, so between tips from the dining room and the snack bar, I made about $2,000 that first summer.

I started work at 6:30 a.m., setting up the dining room, and worked until midnight, cleaning up after the snack bar closed, but I was making what seemed like a fortune for a college kid in 1950.

The next summer I worked at a more upscale place, the Laurels, a hotel and resort on Sackett Lake, in Monticello. My friend Dave Oser came up and worked with me as a busboy. The Laurels had about 1,100 or 1,200 guests. It was a little more expensive than the Kiamesha Lodge, and it had more singles, both men and women. I always got great tips from the women.

Women never stiffed us, but a few times I had to chase guys to make sure we got our tips. Once I went up to a guy as he was checking out and said, "Did you forget something?" "Oh yeah, I was going to come back with your tip," he said. "Well, I'm here now," I replied. I collected, and made sure he also tipped Dave.

The rule of thumb was that guests tipped busboys about half of what the waiters received.

Another time I had to deal with two young guys who I was pretty sure were going to leave without tipping. They were heading out on a Sunday morning right after breakfast, to take advantage of the rush as new guests arrived before lunch. I told Dave to hang around with a full tray of dirty dishes.

When they started to leave, I walked over, blocked their way, and politely reminded them that it was customary to leave a tip. One of the guys said, "Oh, we leave a tip when we feel like leaving a tip."

Between being on the swimming team at Baruch and hauling trays as a waiter, I was in great shape. I leaned toward him and said, "If you don't give us a tip right now, I'm going to tell the busboy to drop that tray of dirty dishes on you."

He said, "You wouldn't." I said, "Absolutely I would." "I'll tell the owner," he said. "Tell him," I said. "You came for a week and you're leaving. He needs me here for the whole summer."

A full program of FUN, SPORTS, and ENTERTAINMENT awaits you at the fabulous Laurels Country Club.

Every activity has been arranged for your pleasure . . . continuous dancing nightly to Latin and American orchestras . . . all-star show . . . free rhumba group instructions . . . television theatre . . . cocktail lounge.

New Buildings Fabulously Furnished Wall to Wall Carpeted. All Rooms with Private Bath and Shower - Phones.

Laurels . .
IS IDEAL
For a Weekend or a Vacation

IT'S NEARER THAN YOU THINK
Only 81 Miles from New York

Ad ad for The Laurels Hotel

Catskills History image

Grudgingly, they pulled out some money. "It's a minimum of twenty apiece," I said. I got the twenties. "Now the busboy." And they paid Dave, too.

I had girlfriends prior to the Catskills, but until those summers, everything was pretty innocent. When I worked at the summer camp I was 18, and had a girlfriend who was only

16. We had a summer romance.

Things were much simpler back then. You walked around, took a canoe ride, did some necking, maybe some petting, but that was about it.

For any of us who worked in the Catskills, what we remember most would be the women. At the Laurels there were a lot of single women, and the management encouraged the waiters, who were all college guys, to ask these single women to dance when we weren't working. In fact, they almost made it mandatory. So I would dance with the women, some of whom were very attractive. Then I would walk them back to their rooms. They were always two in a room.

I'll never forget one woman. She made it pretty clear she was interested in more than dancing, but said, "I really can't bring you in the room, because my friend is there." I thought quickly and said, "Well, what if your friend had a guest?" "Oh, that would be okay."

By now it was 12:30 in the morning. I tell her, "I'll find somebody." I walk out of the room and see a guy walking down the corridor, weaving from side to side. I walk up to him and I say, "Oh, hi, Jack." He says, "No, no, it's Phil." "Oh, yeah, Phil. You looking for your room?" He says, "Yeah, I can't find…" "Where's your key? Oh yeah, I know the room."

I bring him to the girls' room. With the lights off and the door closed, you could barely see the bed. I bring him over to the other bed, where this girl's friend is, and say, "Meet my friend, Phil. He's a nice guy." She says, "Oh yeah, that's great. Hi, Phil." He mumbles, takes off his shirt and pants, and falls into the bed wearing his shorts.

For most of the night I hear this woman saying, "Are you awake, Phil?" It was unbelievable. He slept. I woke up early in the morning to go to work, and they were all sleeping when I left.

I met some wonderful entertainers in the Catskills. Buddy Hackett was just a little bit older than me. Sid Caesar and Imogene Coca came to the Laurels. Red Buttons was there, Gary Moore, Henny Youngman. They all played the Catskills, which at that time was like Vegas is today, except with more places for young comedians and singers, because they didn't get a lot of money. They earned maybe $40 a week.

One of the benefits of being a waiter or busboy was that we could eat anything we wanted, either before or after the meal. Then one day, the general manager decided that we shouldn't have steak. We could have pot roast or chicken, but not steak.

The other waiters and I put our heads together and decided to show him the error of his ways. We all picked up loads of steaks on our trays. An old guy sitting on a stool by the kitchen door was supposed to write down what was on each waiter's tray. He asked me how many entrees I had. I had ten, but said eight. "Well, it looks like..." By the time he got the words out, I was through the door with two guys right behind me, doing the same thing.

The general manager discovered that 1,200 steaks had gone out of the kitchen, but there were only 900 steaks on the old guy's list. Everybody had a steak. After the busboy and I each had steak, we still had two extra because I took so many out. I cut them up as if somebody had eaten them, and threw them out.

My Baruch graduation photo, 1952

The edict lasted maybe a week, and the manager surrendered. We could have steak again. Suddenly the number of steaks leaving the kitchen matched the number counted by the guy at the door.

It had been a foolish decision by the manager anyway, because at that time the difference in cost between a steak and chicken, pot roast or lamb chops was not much. What they charged the guests for them was very different, of course, but the actual food cost was not.

I learned a good lesson from the manager's blunder: treat your help well. As a matter of fact, I treat my employees with more care than I do our customers or our tenants. I want these people to stay with me for years, and they do. Our team is number one. Second in importance, obviously, are the tenants we service. Next are our partners and vendors, whom we treat with great care and regard, because these are the people on whom our livelihood depends.

But number one is our own staff. I learned that in the Catskills.

In the Army Now

In 1952, as college graduation approached, I was thinking about going to law school. I took the LSAT, the Law School Admission Test, and applied to law schools at Harvard, Yale, Columbia, and New York University. I was accepted at all of them. But America was embroiled in the Korean War, and there was a good chance I would be drafted.

A friend suggested I enlist in the Navy, because with a college education I'd become an officer. I decided I'd rather spend three years on a ship than two years in the Army.

I had to take a written test and a physical exam for the Navy. I got something like a 99 on the test, and then went for my physical. Everything went well until the eye test. The doctor asked me to read the same group of numbers four or five times, and I could not get it right. The numbers were in different colors, and there were some colors I couldn't see. I was partially color blind. That meant I could not enlist in the Navy.

After that, I was quickly drafted into the Army. I took Ranger training at Fort Indiantown Gap, Pennsylvania, about 20 miles east of Harrisburg. I had an A profile, which meant physically

I was in great shape. Intellectually I was head and shoulders above the average draftee in the Army, many of whom hadn't finished high school, even though they were drafting some college people. The guys at the camp were all conscripts.

The training was very rigorous. We were there from November through February, the coldest months of the year, and a lot of the time we bivouacked in tents. For us it felt like we were kidding around, because we were all healthy and strong. We had to do pushups the right way, which meant staying parallel to the ground. I could do 100 at a time. They made me a platoon guide, which was a training helper to the sergeant. There were about 80 of us in our group. As a platoon guide I marched alongside the other troops, with the training sergeant leading the way.

Our training sergeant was pretty formidable. He was about six two, probably 240 pounds. He had lost an eye in combat in Korea, and wore a big eye patch.

He encouraged me to go to Officers Candidate School because he knew I had done well in the Navy test except for being color blind. Our commanding officer also urged me to go to OCS. I didn't want to, because if I went into OCS from a combat training group like ours, I'd have ended up as a second lieutenant leading troops into frontline fighting in Korea. I didn't want to be a killer, shooting at people and having somebody shooting at me and my troops.

Going into the second month of training camp, in December, I began coughing. I took some cough medicine, but over the next couple of days it got worse. On the third day I told the sergeant I thought I should go on sick call.

The Army made it difficult to go on sick call, because they didn't want guys saying they had to see the doctor just so they could get out of training for half a day. So, to go on sick call, you had to take everything you had, put it into your footlocker, bring your footlocker to the supply building, and have it stored there. Then you went to the doctor. When you were done, you got your footlocker out of storage, brought it back to your barracks, and unpacked.

That was more of a hassle than I wanted to deal with, so I didn't go to the doctor.

After a week, I started falling behind on our marches, and began to spit up blood. I had an idea. You didn't have to go through the whole pack-store-unpack rigmarole if you wanted to go to a dentist. So I told the sergeant, "I have a terrible toothache." He let me go to the dentist.

When I got there, I sat in the chair and the nurse put one of those napkins on me. The dentist came in and said, "What seems to be the problem?"

Before I could say anything, I started to cough, and the whole napkin was covered with blood. The dentist said, "You've got to go to the doctor. I can't do anything for you."

I went next door, and the doctor listened to my chest. An X-ray confirmed that I had pneumonia. At that time there was very little they could do; the pneumonia just had to play itself out.

I stayed in the hospital for

In the Army, 1953

almost a month, after which they sent me home on sick leave for another month. When I returned from the leave, my unit was gone, dispatched to various parts of the world. Probably 95% went to the front in Korea, and the rest to Japan and Germany.

I was back in the same barracks. It was eerie to be there. It usually held 80 troops, but the only other people there were three guys from Brooklyn who had gone AWOL, absent without leave. To me they seemed like street thugs. Rather than put them in the brig, the base officers decided to have them finish training, after which they'd be sent to the front in Korea.

The training sergeant was not happy, because instead of getting his usual three- or four-week break between platoons, he had to run us through all the training situations we hadn't covered. That meant teaching us to throw hand grenades, operate mortars, and how to use a Browning Automatic Rifle or BAR, night scopes and almost every other weapon or piece of equipment the Army had. We took special classes in hand-to-hand combat and how to kill people with everything from knives to shoelaces.

The sergeant was annoyed that he had to teach the four of us, because in his mind, we were all shirkers. It was no use explaining to the sergeant that I had been sick. He lumped me in with the three guys who had gone AWOL. Every afternoon he reverted to what he usually did when there was no training: get drunk.

Lights out in the barracks was at nine o'clock. Sometime around midnight there'd be a shake on my bunk. I'd open my eyes to see a six-foot-two guy with a big eyepatch shouting, "I'm going to get you, Field." I knew he was drunk, but that didn't make it any less frightening. I began sleeping with a bayonet in bed. I decided to do something, and fast.

I went to see the captain, but he was away. I said to his clerk, "I want to get out of here. I'd like to go to a school near New York. What is there?" He looked it up. "The closest school is Fort Slocum." It was close to New Rochelle, next to the Glen Island casino where Glenn Miller used to play. The clerk said it had a school for field grade officers, a school for chaplains, and an information educational school.

I said, "What's this information education?" "Well," he said, "the information class teaches you how to be a reporter for *Stars and Stripes,* or just to report on wherever you're stationed. You give news releases to the local papers and to the stateside papers." Having written for *The Ticker* at Baruch, I liked that.

"What about the education part?" He explained that we'd get training so we could give classes at whatever base we were sent to, on whatever subject the Army decided we should teach. We might give a class in English or Spanish or history, for soldiers who hadn't finished high school.

I said, "That's great. I like that idea. I'll go there." The clerk was hesitant. "I don't know if the captain will sign the papers for you to go. I'll have to talk to him about it."

I asked him when the next class started at Fort Slocum. This was a Tuesday, and when he checked he discovered that the next class started on the following Monday, and lasted for six weeks.

"I have to go now," I said. "I can't wait six weeks for the next course." I pleaded that I might get killed by the three guys in the barracks or the sergeant. Then I handed him $20, and he filled out the papers.

The clerk was still doubtful, saying the captain might not approve the transfer. I told him to stick the paperwork in the middle of the stack, and the captain would probably sign it without even reading it. If he did question the transfer, the clerk could just say I had lied to him and told him it had been approved.

What's the worst that can happen? "The captain is going to think that this wise guy from New York came in and conned you into thinking that he said it was okay to do it." There wasn't much risk to me, because no officer would want to go through the red tape of writing up a charge against me, and without the transfer I'd be on my way to Korea anyway.

Two days later, on Thursday, the training clerk told me the captain had signed the paperwork. The class at Fort Slocum started on Monday, so my orders said I was to leave the next day.

That night I packed up everything in my duffle bag. The sergeant usually came around at 8:30 a.m., so an hour and a half before that I grabbed my bag and took a bus to town, then boarded another bus to New York City. I never saw the sergeant or the three AWOL guys again.

My escape to New York gave me confidence that I could handle difficult situations. I didn't have to be blown around by chance.

I went back to the Bronx for the weekend. My mother and

father were overjoyed that, for at least a little while, I was going to be in New Rochelle, just 15 miles away.

By now they had two cars. My mother hardly ever used hers. Nobody wanted her to drive, because she was a menace behind the wheel. She took her driving test eight times, and only passed it when my father gave the inspector $50, which was a gigantic sum back then. So they lent me her car to use while I was at Fort Slocum.

The base looked like a college campus. If someone had put ivy on the buildings, you would have thought they were dorms. It had a "permanent party," the Army term for a staff, of about 150 people who taught classes and ran the place. Classes of students arrived every six to eight weeks, then left and were replaced by the next group.

The base commander's position rotated every two years, with a senior officer from the Army, Navy or Air Force taking the post. A Navy admiral was in charge when I arrived. The barracks were two- and three-story buildings.

Each "information education" class had 140 or 150 men. There were about 20 there for the chaplain school, and a smaller number of field grade officers – majors, lieutenant colonels and colonels – taking other classes. So the whole post was very small, about 350 people in all.

The classes were relatively simple for anybody who had gone to college. In fact, the majority of my fellow classmates had a college, master's or doctorate degree, because many of them had stayed in school as long as possible to avoid being drafted.

Our class taught us to write as journalists. The experience was helpful later, because it made it easy for me to write marketing information about my buildings, draft letters to mortgage companies, and manage other business communication.

The approach they taught us was simple: put all the key information – who, what, why, when and where – in the first paragraph, and then add the details of the story, so you have a beginning, middle and an end. Between my experience at the *Ticker* and writing courses I had taken in college, it was pretty simple for me.

They would give us a few pages of information about

something that happened — for example, a train wreck in which somebody was killed and some other people were injured, plus a few other details. Then we had an hour to write the news story. Between being a pretty good writer and a decent touch typist, the assignment usually took me only 20 minutes, maybe 30 if I dawdled.

One of the guys who sat next to me in class was also from the Bronx. He was a driver in the motor pool, and hadn't gone to college. His name was Hank Popowicz, which he later changed to Hank Paul. I'd glance over at Hank after finishing my story, and he'd still be reading the three pages that he's supposed to write about.

I asked him why he wasn't writing, and he said he didn't understand how to write a news story. I tried to explain, but he didn't get it. Finally I put a new sheet of paper in my typewriter, wrote another story, and handed it to him.

Hank and I became friends. We fell into a pattern of my doing his stories as well as mine. He was such a nice guy that I didn't mind. It was a mitzvah, a good deed.

We remained very friendly after we left the Army. Later, we volunteered with the Bronx Junior Chamber of Commerce, helping to build a house for a family with triplets, all of whom had been blind since birth. He was always a good person in my book.

If I can help people who need a hand, and they're sincere, I have no qualms about going out of my way. I enjoy helping or mentoring people. I keep reminding myself that something with which I'm very familiar can be new to other people, just as there are many things that are new to me.

In the case of Hank Paul, I gave him a little help, and in return gained a decades-long friendship with a great guy.

Classes at Fort Slocum ran Monday to Friday. With my mother's car, I was able to go home every weekend. A lot of the guys were from other parts of the country, so I'd take a couple of them with me. To them, I was the big New Yorker.

In fact, as a Bronx boy, New Rochelle and the Westchester County area was a foreign country to me. But my friends didn't know that. "Larry's a New Yorker, he'll know where to go." So I usually ended up taking them to the Bronx, which I knew well.

We'd go to Amerigo's, on Tremont Avenue, my favorite pizza place. I admit I liked showing the guys I grew up with, some of whom used to chase me when we were kids, that I was now in the Army and had new friends.

Six weeks passed quickly, and my class waited for our orders. Everyone received their assignments except me. I went to see the warrant officer in charge. "We don't have your orders yet, Larry." Every day or two I would ask him when I would get orders. After a week, when a new class was about to start, he told me there was a mix-up in my papers.

Apparently I was supposed to have been sent back to Fort Indiantown Gap, or reassigned from Fort Slocum, but neither had been done. And they couldn't simply redo the paperwork at Fort Slocum. Because the base was jointly overseen by the Army, Navy and Air Force, any change in my orders had to be done through the Department of the Army, in Washington.

How long would that take? Nobody was certain, but a clerk guessed it could take a month or more. So I waited.

They didn't give me a job at first, so every day I'd get up, go to the gym, do some exercises, maybe play some volleyball or basketball. I met a Marine Corps captain from Camp Lejeune, in North Carolina, who was playing badminton. I'd only seen the game in the movies, being played by women in white skirts. I never knew there was competitive badminton. He taught me to play, and soon we were playing every afternoon after his classes, and little by little I got really good at it.

The armed forces encourages base commanders to field sports teams, because being a soldier can be pretty boring when you are not in battle. You have a job, you train, you march, every once in a while you shoot a gun, but outside of that there's not a lot to do.

The marine captain happened to mention to the base commander that this guy, Private Field, was a competitive badminton player. By now it was three weeks after the rest of my group had left.

The admiral called me in and said, "Private Field, I know nobody is quite sure what to do with you. There's a tennis and badminton tournament. Would you like to go?" "Sure."

The captain and I went. If you went to a tournament, which

usually started on a Monday, they let you go on the prior Saturday, and you didn't have to be back to the base until a week from that Monday, a whole nine days. I think we lost our matches and were out of the tournament by Wednesday, so I went home to the Bronx.

When I was back on base, the admiral called me again. "Private Field, as long as you're here, I'd like you to be the manager of the various teams we field to go to these tournaments." "Sure." "Do you play tennis?" "I did, but not well. "How about basketball?" Of course. I had gone to City College, which had a great basketball team.

He ran the gamut: baseball, tennis, golf, softball, skeet shooting, track and field. I only said no to track and field; I knew next to nothing about them. So I became the manager of all the teams.

A couple of days later the admiral said, "There's a tennis tournament at West Point. You need six players." I was one, and I found five other guys. I'd tell them, "You want a week off to play tennis? You don't know how to play? I'll teach you."

The tennis team left on a Saturday, arrived at West Point on Monday, and was eliminated on Tuesday. We lost every match, singles and doubles. We had the rest of the week for ourselves. We did the same thing with basketball. We were always eliminated by the second day.

The admiral thought it was wonderful. I found out it didn't matter about winning. If a post had less than 1,000 people, it got the same credit for just showing up as if its team came in third or fourth. In fact, the admiral won some awards for fielding all these teams.

Periodically I asked the warrant officer about my orders. After a month, I volunteered for Europe. He said, "I'll put it down, Field, but I doubt it. Everybody wants to go to Europe." Two weeks later I asked to go to Japan, but he said a lot of people volunteered for Japan.

After six weeks, I said, "I'll go anywhere." I knew that even if I got sent to Korea I wouldn't be a frontline soldier, because I now had the designation of information education person. I'd be on the base newspaper, or I'd be a correspondent for the *Stars and Stripes*.

In the eighth week he said, "Well, I did find out something. The admiral requested that you remain here as permanent party," meaning I would be a member of the base staff.

I was incredulous. The officer explained that my paperwork had been bouncing from desk to desk at the Department of the Army, then to the Department of Defense, then back. Nobody wanted to make a decision. When the admiral asked to have me permanently assigned to Fort Slocum, that solved the paperwork problem for them.

The admiral called me in. "Private Field, I'm going to recommend a promotion for you. You should be a corporal, because if you're going to be here as permanent party, the best thing for you to do is to be an instructor."

He asked what I had studied in college. I told him I had majored in business and minored in public administration and political science.

"Ah, political science. Do you know about Communism?" Of course I did. "Okay, you're going to teach geopolitical science, mainly about Communism. You're going to teach field grade officers. We'll give you a light load. You only have to teach two hours a day — ten hours a week. That way you can keep doing the teams."

He didn't want the teaching to interfere with me being team manager. If anyone wanted to play any sport, they had to see me. So, because of a paperwork snafu I got to stay on the post, teaching classes and fielding teams.

I soon discovered that when I was introduced as the instructor, the officers in my classes assumed I knew what I was talking about, just as the students had when I was teaching at Dale Carnegie. In fact, I used my Dale Carnegie training when I taught my Army classes.

Many of the men had more military training than I had, and some were college graduates. But I studied hard for the first class, staying a chapter ahead of the students, and was fine. After the first session, I gave the same lectures to the next group, so I really mastered the subject. There was a new class every eight weeks; six weeks of classes plus a two-week hiatus.

I got very friendly with the doctor on the post. We'd play chess together at his quarters after dinner. One evening a phone call interrupted our chess game. I heard him say, "Gee, I didn't think she was due for another ten days. I'll be right over."

He hung up and said, "Field, come with me." He explained that a captain's wife was expecting their third child, it was arriving early, and we had to drive her to the ferry.

When we got to the captain's home, the doctor went into the bedroom, then came back out. "Larry, I want you to help me. We can't take her to the ferry. The baby is halfway out. Go wash your hands, get some sheets, and come in, just in case there's a problem."

I said I thought it would be better to have her husband help, but the doctor said the husband would be too nervous. "What I want you to do is hold these sheets. When the baby comes out, it'll be bloody and covered with the placenta. Wipe it off as much as you can. I'll cut the umbilical cord. Okay? Everything'll be fine. This is her third child, she'll be okay."

He was right, and the delivery was very quick. I helped clean up the baby, and the doctor did the rest, gave the baby to the mother, and called in the father. In all we were there for about two and a half hours. Seeing a baby being born was amazing.

I never thought about making a career of the Army, because I knew the Army way of life was not for me. I didn't mind discipline, because that can be enjoyable. You know your obligations and boundaries, you're taken care of, you get clothing, food, housing. It's not so bad when you think of it that way. But I knew I would never be able to deal with the bureaucracy.

I didn't know what career I wanted to pursue; I just was sure I wanted to get away from the grocery store and the little apartments. We never owned a home. My father always rented in a two-family house. I wanted to get away from that.

When my time was up and I got out of the Army, I was happy to be on my own again. My two years in uniform had created a clean break from home, and instilled a great deal of confidence in me. When I left the Army I was 22, almost 23, and my time in the service was a very important part of my training for life. I'll always be grateful for the opportunity it gave me to grow and become a real adult, my own man.

After I was discharged, my Army buddy Hank Popowicz got

me involved with the Bronx Junior Chamber of Commerce. It was building a home in Throggs Neck for a family with triplets who had been accidentally blinded right after they were born.

They were born prematurely and placed in an incubator that had a high concentration of oxygen, which was the accepted way at the time to deal with the respiratory problems common with preemies. It was not until the mid-1950s that Dr. Arnall Patz proved that the oxygen therapy caused blindness.

By then, some 10,000 infants had lost their sight, including Frank and Marie Petraglia's triplets. Building a house for them took a little over a year, and it was a wonderful experience. I was involved hands-on with something very real and tangible, and life-changing for the Petraglia family.

In 1955, I took my first job after the Army, for a public relations company. It was sort of related to news and journalism, and I thought I'd like that. One of the accounts was a diaper company. The owner of the agency said to me, "We made this giant diaper. The circus is in town. We want you to go down to the circus and get a really good picture of a baby elephant wearing the diaper."

I called the Ringling Bros. and Barnum and Bailey Circus. They liked the idea, because they'd get publicity. A photographer and I went to Madison Square Garden and down to the basement, where they kept the animals. They had probably 25 elephants there.

We picked out a baby, and took her aside to diaper her. It wasn't easy, because even a baby elephant is pretty big, and the adult elephants began trumpeting as if to say, "Why are you taking away this baby?" We got the diaper on the elephant and took a picture.

This, I realized, was not a career for me. I left the PR company after about five months.

My next job was with Hazel Bishop, a cosmetics company, selling lipsticks to drugstores. They were competing with Revlon, which at the time was the big lipstick brand.

It turned out that some of their senior sales people were running a crooked scheme. They shipped cartons of merchandise to salesmen that we hadn't requested. I couldn't understand why I was getting all these shipments – 15 or 20 cases at a time.

I had nowhere to put them, so I had them shipped to my father's store, which had a basement for storage. My father kept a careful record of the shipments, as he did with all of his goods.

It turned out that the scheme was simple. They would tell the company that they sent a salesman – say Larry Field – 30 cases, but they'd only send 15. They would keep the rest of the merchandise, sell it for half price, and pocket the money.

The company eventually discovered the scheme. Then an investigator showed up at my father's store, demanding to see the 30 cases. My father produced the shipping receipts, which showed that only 15 cases had been delivered. The schemers got fired, along with everyone else. They fired me, they fired everybody. The company figured they'd start over.

By this time it was late in 1955. I was again living with my folks, which after the freedom of being in the Army was not very appealing. I was determined to find a job that would take me out of New York City. The job that would do that was with Lever Brothers, and my life would never be the same.

Lever Brothers – Getting Started

I answered a Help Wanted ad looking for college graduates to work out of town. It had been placed by Lever Brothers, a huge soap-making company that today is known as Unilever. I was told to go to Lever House, a glass skyscraper at 390 Park Avenue that had just opened a couple of years earlier.

I was interviewed for a few minutes, and they said, "Well, you're hired. Can you start in two days?" "Sure." If I had been more experienced, I would have realized that they were probably just hiring any warm body with a college diploma.

The interview was on a Tuesday. Two days later I flew to Chicago, to meet the others on the sales crew I'd be joining. I was met at the airport by a supervisor, who brought me to a motel where 19 other salesmen, all with college degrees from various schools, were staying; I was the twentieth. We each had a motel room, and each got a station wagon.

We had been hired to introduce a new, luxury line of soap called Dove. It would be launched in Chicago because Lever

Brothers had a big soap factory in Hammond, Indiana, about 25 miles away.

We would drive to Hammond, load our station wagons with soap, and then make our sales calls. Every day the supervisor would give us a list of 12 to 15 grocery stores. Our goal was to sell each of them a case of soap.

There were two sizes of Dove soap, large and small. They were very expensive. The large one sold for 25 cents, and the small one for 15. At the time, bars of Lux and Ivory soap sold for a nickel, maybe less.

Lever Brothers took a page from Proctor & Gamble's marketing book, because P&G was the best at introducing new products. Rather than just running newspaper and television ads, P&G sent salespeople out to all the stores, making sure merchandise was on store shelves when its ads broke.

The large retailers, including supermarket and grocery chains as well as co-ops, cooperative buying groups of independent stores, all made their purchasing decisions at the headquarters level. But the owners of little stores would only stock an item after their customers asked for it. Lever Brothers wanted Dove in these little stores when people came in.

I had a big advantage because, having worked in my father's little grocery store, I understood the thinking of the store owners. I never failed to sell something to a grocer. The stores were basically the same size as my father's, and the owners did everything, working hard for 12 hours a day.

The first thing they said was, "Too expensive." These small stores would never take a case of soap. I'd say, "Fine, take six bars of each." If that was too much, I'd tell them to take three of each.

I wouldn't leave. I would tell them, "You know, my father has a store just like this in the Bronx. I know how hard you work. But this has the highest profit of any item you're going to sell in your store. You're going to make five cents on each bar of Dove." They were making a penny on a bar of Lux, maybe less. I always sold them something, without exception.

A week went by, and I was getting restless. I would finish calling on the stores on my list by 10 a.m., 11 at the latest, and didn't know what to do. I couldn't stand the idea of going to a movie in the daytime.

I began looking around the Chicago area for big stores, independent supermarkets. I'd go in and speak to the owner. He would be shocked by the cost of the soap, and more shocked when I told him that Jewel, a big supermarket chain in Chicago, and A&P, a national chain, were going to put 100 cases in every store.

The soap that changed my life

M. F. Ramli photo

I didn't really know that they were going to put in 100 cases. Our supervisor said he was trying to get the big chains to put 50 to a 100 cases in the store.

The owners I was talking to would say, "Oh, that's too much. I can't afford 100 cases."

I said, "Well, if you buy 100 cases, I'll have the truck from Hammond deliver tomorrow, and I'll meet it here stack it for you, so your employees don't have to do that. And I'll give you $100 dollars in cash, a dollar a case, for advertising allowance."

Then I would tell them that the supermarkets that took those 100 cases per store were doing very well.

The owners almost always had one last question: "What if it doesn't sell?" I told them that I would be placing the order through their cooperative, not them. If the soap doesn't sell, the cooperative was not going to pay Lever Brothers, because the co-op hadn't placed the order. Second, if Dove didn't sell at their store, it would not sell at Jewel or A&P. If Dove was a failure, Lever Brothers would absorb the loss rather than alienate the stores that sold a lot of its other products.

So there was really no risk for him or his store, he was getting $100 for advertising, and I would set up the display for him.

I never missed on these sales.

I had been doing this for a little over three weeks when the supervisor called me in. He said he had to go to New York for a meeting, and was putting me in charge of the team.

I said, "Why me? I was the last to arrive here." He told me, "Look, there's you and 19 other guys, and you've sold more soap than all of them put together. You've sold over 800 cases in the last three weeks. None of the others have sold more than 10 cases. You're obviously doing something right."

I was very proud to be put in charge. I really had no idea I was that good a salesman; you could say my success took me by surprise. Now, instead of just being one of many salesmen, I'd be leading other men. It sounded great to me. I couldn't wait to get started.

It turned out that being in charge was no big deal. My salary didn't change. All it meant was that I handed out the routes for the other 19 guys. The good thing, though, was that I called on the few chain stores, drug and grocery chains and co-ops, that the supervisor hadn't visited yet. I could stop going to the individual stores.

A week passed, and the supervisor didn't come back. He got promoted — probably because of my great salesmanship! I got a call from a vice president in New York who said, "Larry, you're doing such a good job that we're going to leave you in charge."

Then he told me the plan was changing. It didn't make sense to send a team of 20 guys to other cities. Instead, they would fly me and five salesmen to one state at a time. I'd take the largest city, and send the others to smaller markets. We'd all call on the large drug and grocery chains, not the small independent stores.

I thought this was great. It was really my first job of any significance. I didn't even think about what I would be getting paid. It turned out I'd be getting the same $125 a week.

As we went around the country, I got better and better at selling. I found that if you treat people like you would want to be treated, they want to help you and do business with you or buy from you. If they feel that you're part of the decision with them, they'll go with your recommendation and buy, every time.

I never let it be a question of whether they should buy or not buy. It was if they should buy 100 cases per store or 50 cases. I would participate with them in that decision.

The best sales I got were when the buyer, who usually was a vice president because these were big orders, would say to me, "Well, what do you

Traveling the country for Lever Brothers

think, Larry? How much would you buy if you were me?" I'd say, "There's no question that I would buy the hundred cases a store. You have nothing to lose." In fact, that was true.

The clincher was the advertising allowance of a dollar per case. Let's say a chain had 100 stores, and ordered 100 cases per store. They would get a $100 per store in advertising allowance, which for 100 stores was $10,000.

I'd write a check for $10,000 and hand it to him. The question always was, what happens if they have to send back some of the soap. "You keep the money." That's how it worked.

I learned that most people want to help you if you're a nice guy and you approach them in a way that makes them feel comfortable. If you can do that, you can sell them almost anything. That was a good lesson.

Of course, to get to see the right person, sometimes I'd have to be really obnoxious and insist upon seeing the vice president in charge of sales, or the president of the company. I needed somebody much higher up than the normal buyer of soap.

I realized that I usually got an audience with somebody other than the buyer because I was with Lever Brothers. If it was just Larry Field asking to see them, I probably wouldn't get in. But I would still give them a reason. I'd say, "It's important that I see this person because the amount that we're talking about is so large."

When I saw them in their office, I'd look around. I might see photos on the wall of the guy with politicians or other important people, or of a fish or a sailboat, or there might be a trophy on a shelf or a plaque on the wall. I'd ask him about that object, and how they came to get it. All you have to do is ask a few questions, and he's telling you a story.

It's important to really listen. Most people don't listen closely. If a person feels you are really interested in what he's saying, the conversation will go on for quite a while. Usually when I'd walk in the executive would say, "I can only give you five minutes." Well, soon it's 15 minutes, and we haven't even talked about Dove soap.

Eventually he'd say, "Well, tell me what you got." He knew I was with Lever Brothers, but he didn't know what I was selling. So I'd take out the samples, tell him how much it cost, tell him Lever Brothers was going to spend $5 million next month on TV ads in his area, and tell him that other big chains were taking 100 cases per store and making a lot of money.

Then I'd tell him that I, Larry Field, was going to write him a check for $100 per store. "You have 400 stores, so that's $40,000. I'll write the check right now."

This approach always worked, because the product and offer were sound, and because I created a relationship with the guy. I enjoyed meeting people, and I think people recognized that I was really interested in them – why, for example, he had a model ship on his desk.

Sometimes the men I met (at the time these jobs were always held by men) would ask me why I bothered to ask about the personal stuff we discussed, because I was only passing through. I was honest. "Odds are I will not see you again in my whole life, but while we're together, it's interesting for me to know a little bit more about you. I think it's great for both of us."

It certainly was great for Lever Brothers, because I sold about $15 million of Dove soap for the company, when the regular salesmen calling on drugstores were selling maybe $250,000 a year. I was the fair-haired boy of the company. I could do no wrong.

And that eventually turned out to be my biggest problem.

On the Road: My Secret Method For Meeting People

Going from city to city made for a pretty lonely existence, especially on the weekends. I tried going to bars to meet people, but I couldn't handle more than two drinks a night. I finally came up with an ingenious method for meeting people on the road.

I'd put six or eight bars of soap in my briefcase, drive to a nice section of town, and go into the biggest drugstore I could find. Even in the South and Midwest, at least half of the larger drugstores were owned by Jews. I'd look at the front of the store to see the pharmacist's name. Usually it would be Irving Cohen, registered pharmacist, Harry Berkowitz, registered pharmacist, and so on.

I'd go in, looking like a salesman, in a jacket and tie. I'd go up to the pharmacist and say, "Mr. Berkowitz?" "Yes?" "I'm with Lever Brothers." "Oh. You should see the girl. She buys the notions." "No, no, I have to see you." "I'm busy doing prescriptions."

I said, "Well, I'll wait. I'm sure you take a break once in a while." "I'll be busy for a couple of hours." "That's okay. I don't have much to do. I'll wait."

I'd pull up a chair and sit, making sure he could see me.

It's very disconcerting to see a person waiting for you, because you know you can stop for five minutes. It was never more than 15 minutes, and usually less than five, before he would relent and come down, angry. I'd take out my soap. "Oh my God, I don't buy soap."

I said, "It's not soap. It's very expensive. It's something you should have. You've got probably one of the nicest drugstores in town. Women are going to buy this, big time. All the supermarkets in town are going to have it. They're going to have displays of it. And you should have it. You don't want to be left behind."

I would explain that it had no lye, it had cold cream. "After all, you're a professional in the medical field. You know what lye does to your skin." I'd go through the whole spiel.

He'd say, "All right, how much is it?" I'd tell him the large bar was 25 cents, the small one was 15. "My God, that's too expensive. I only pay four cents for Lux or Ivory." "But they're not going to advertise like this. And they're a different kind of soap. The highest class women in town are going to come in to buy this." "Oh gee, I don't know."

I said, "Look, I can't leave your store unless you buy minimum three bars of each. You should buy more, because you've got a big store here. But I'll settle for three of each. It would be a disservice to you."

He'd say, "What, you mean you won't leave?" I said, "No, I won't. I'll go back and sit on that chair again."

It never failed. "All right, all right. I'll buy it." Six bars of soap were 90 cents; he could get rid of me for less than a dollar.

Now, at that time, I had blond hair, I was 165 pounds, in great shape, working for Lever Brothers with a name like Larry Field – all very non-Jewish.

I'd say to him, "Is there a synagogue in town?" Invariably it would be almost like I pushed him. He'd be taken aback. It was always the same reaction. I'd add, "It's Friday, and I'd like go to services this evening or tomorrow."

"Oh, sure. Wait a minute." Then he'd go back to his work

area and get on the phone to his wife. "There's a handsome young guy here who's with Lever Brothers, he's Jewish, and he wants to go to services."

In small cities and towns, the temple or synagogue were – and mostly still are – the center of the Jewish community's social life. This goes for any place in the world. If you are Jewish and want to meet some people in any country where there are Jews, go find the synagogue. You'll be accepted.

It was a great entrée for me. I would always meet people. At least half the time, maybe three quarters, I was invited to dinner that evening by somebody. It might not be the pharmacist, but it would be somebody with a daughter or niece or somebody single.

I'd get a dinner, then we'd go to temple, where everybody came around to say hello. I would be asked by the men and women my age to join them in some activity the next day, on Saturday – a picnic, water skiing, whatever was doing in that town.

I always enjoyed meeting new people, and it was far better meeting them at the synagogue than at a bar.

Our sales team went into Virginia, then Ohio, Georgia, Mississippi and Alabama. After a few months, they cut the group from five plus me to three plus me. We'd fly in, I'd take the biggest city in the state, and send the other three to smaller cities.

Then Lever Brothers called a regional sales meeting in St. Louis, for the sales people, district managers, sales managers and regional managers – about 150 in all. It was about introducing Dove to individual drug and grocery stores. At the end of the meeting the regional manager handed me the bill, which was for several thousand dollars. We didn't have credit cards; we paid for everything with cash or checks.

The manager said headquarters would approve the expense, because it had sent out a bulletin to all the regional managers in the United States that whenever Larry Field was in their territory and they had a regional meeting, any expense he incurred would be approved automatically. I was pretty impressed with myself.

Then I began asking questions.

I found out that the salesmen calling on drugstores for products like Pepsodent toothpaste got $125 a week plus a company car. I was making $125 a week, plus a rental car. I asked what their annual sales were, and learned that the average was about $200,000, and about $250,000 for a really good salesman.

At this point, I had sold millions of dollars of Dove soap in about five months. My paycheck was about $500 a month, and my expense checks were $10,000 a month for cars, trains, plane trips and hotels, and as much as $30,000 if we had a regional sales meeting. At the time, $30,000 was a fortune. A new Chevrolet sold for less than $1,900.

It was clear I wasn't ever going to be the president of Lever Brothers.

Until a few years earlier, Charles Luckman had been president of the company. He was a Jewish guy from Chicago. He had trained as an architect, but couldn't make a living at that, so he went to work for Pepsodent toothpaste. He rose through the ranks and, at the height of the depression, 1936, '37 and '38, he was selling carloads of Pepsodent toothpaste. The press called him "the boy wonder of American Business."

Lever Brothers wanted the product and him, so they bought the Pepsodent company and made Luckman general sales manager, and then, at age 37, president of Lever Brothers USA. Its headquarters then was in Boston.

The story I heard was that he wanted to join a country club in Boston, but they wouldn't let him in because he was Jewish. Supposedly, that's why he moved the headquarters to New York City, which is how Lever House came into being.

He was a very flamboyant guy. He flew in a private plane and hung around with Zsa Zsa Gabor and other actresses. Lever Brothers was a very staid company, so they must have been a bit embarrassed by him. He went back to being an architect in 1950.

With Luckman in their recent past, I didn't think Lever Brothers would rush to make another Jewish guy, Larry Field, president of the company.

Time to Quit

Every Sunday I'd fly into a different city, and fly out the following Sunday for the next city. After six months, I called up the sales vice president who had told me about my big promotion, and I told him I was quitting. The schedule was wearing me down, and I was not earning enough money.

I was heading to Atlanta, and he flew there to convince me to stay. "You got a great career here, you're fabulous." He tells me to go to Miami, by myself, for a week. There were only seven accounts there, which I could cover in a day or two, and I could relax for the rest of the week.

I went, and it was wonderful. I took it easy, met some interesting women, and relaxed. It was like R&R, rest and recuperation, in the military.

The good feelings didn't last. I decided to stay with Lever Brothers until the end of the campaign to introduce Dove.

I ended up in New Mexico, exhausted. I took off for three days, flying to Mexico for some fishing. When I got back to the New Mexico motel where I was staying, there was a stack of messages from the office, wanting to know where I was.

I sent in my report saying I had been in Baja California, and put the airfare on my expense account.

They didn't say a word. I realized my salary was so low they didn't care what I did or spent.

The idea of working my way up the ladder at Lever Brothers, hoping to wind up as a middle manager, wasn't for me. If I couldn't get to be president, I wasn't interested.

The vice president who had flown to meet me in Atlanta and told me what a great future I had with the company was about 10 years older than me. He left the company a few months after giving me that pep talk. He got an offer to be president of an advertising agency.

I thought to myself, he's telling me what a great company it is, what a great future I had, and he left to go somewhere else? I had to get out of there.

I thought about what I should do. I figured I had to go into a business that didn't require a lot of capital, because I didn't have much.

One option was insurance, another was securities, and a third was real estate. I didn't know much about insurance, except the 25 cents a week my father paid to the insurance agent for his life insurance. I knew even less about selling stocks, bonds and other securities, and nothing about real estate.

But first I had to finish up what I was doing for Lever Brothers. My plan was to get them to fire me, so I could collect unemployment insurance. Then I would take a trip to Europe, come back, and find a new job.

So how was I going to get them to fire me?

We had to send in a sales report every week. One week I worked every day. The next week I put down in my report that I worked only three days, Monday, Wednesday, and Friday.

I don't hear anything.

The third week, I put down that I worked only Tuesday and Thursday. I still didn't hear from anybody.

The fourth week I reported that I hadn't done anything at all. Meanwhile, they're still sending me my paycheck. Not a sound.

I couldn't stand it. I called up the district manager, a guy named Al Gobart, and said I had to bring in my sales report and talk to him. His office was on 42nd Street, off Fifth Avenue. I give him the report, which said I had done no work that whole week.

He looks at it and says, "Oh, okay. What did you want to discuss with me, Larry?" I said, "Al, did you notice that in the last few weeks I worked three days one week, then two, and now none?" He says, "Yeah, I see."

Then he said, "Look, Larry, if you're trying to get me to fire you, you've got a lost cause." "Why?" "You sold $15 million dollars' worth of Dove soap. You could do no work for the next 10 years and it won't mean anything to the company."

He said he couldn't fire me even if he wanted to, because he'd have to explain why he fired the star salesman. "I'm married, I have kids, I don't want to lose my job." He said that if I wanted somebody to fire me, I'd have to get the president of the division to do it.

I sat there, stunned. My great plan wouldn't work. So, unable to get fired from Lever Brothers, I quit.

Because I'd left voluntarily, I had to wait six weeks before I started receiving unemployment insurance.

I took a trip to Cuba, which was very interesting. This was five years before the Cuban Missile Crisis, after which Cuba was closed to Americans.

Then I headed for Europe, traveling alone. It turned out to be a great experience, because I could just pick up on the spur of the moment and go where I liked.

The Aviation Club and My First International Deal

A fter traveling around several countries, my last stop was Paris. I met a group of young people who were traveling together, and I went out with one of the girls.

The next day she said to me, "My girlfriend has a date with this Texas oilman, and she asked us if we wanted to go with them." I said, "Sure." Remember, I had quit my job, and my budget for going out with a girl was maybe $10 – for drinks, dinner and a cab. So I was a little nervous about double-dating with a Texas oilman.

We met him at the Aviation Club de France, on the Champs-Élysées. The Aviation Club had nothing to do with aviation; it was a world-famous gambling club and casino. It was quite exclusive; we had to wait at the entrance until he came out to escort us inside. He was 45 to 50, which to me at 27 seemed pretty old, but he was very friendly. "Well, maybe we should go to the Crazy Horse for dinner and drinks," he said.

I knew that the Crazy Horse, a cabaret, was a rip-off and strictly for tourists. I had been thinking we'd go to one of the

Left Bank places that were a lot cheaper.

I pulled him off to the side and said, "Look, I've got $20. I can't afford a place like that, and I don't want to go under false pretenses and not be able to pay my end when the bill comes." "No problem," he says, "we'll eat here. It's a great place."

We go into the dining room, and he introduces me and the two girls to the maître d' as his guests. We had a fabulous meal: chateaubriand, two kinds of wine, anything you could want.

"Gee, this must be very expensive," I said to him. "No, it's free. You have to be a member of the club, and you have to gamble."

He took us into the casino where the three of us watched him play baccarat, where he quickly lost about $1,000. Then he offered to sign me up as a temporary member of the club, which I gratefully accepted.

The next day I had a date with a different girl, and we doubledated with another couple. I took us back to the Aviation Club, and we again had a wonderful meal, nice wines, the whole thing.

I had brought $50 with me and played some baccarat, making $5 bets and making sure I about broke even. It was another successful evening.

The third day I did the same thing, with the same girl, bringing a different couple with us. Again we had a terrific meal, fine wines and so on.

But this time I get a bill, for $150. That was an incredible amount of money in 1957. I ask the waiter, "What is this bill for?" Suddenly he doesn't speak English.

The manager comes over, and I ask to see him alone. We walk to the side. I said, "I don't understand this. My friend so-and-so told me that you don't charge for meals. You just have to be a member of the club."

That was true, he said, but they had seen that I had only gambled a small amount. They knew what I was doing, and they were going to charge me for the meal.

"Well, I have to tell you something," I said. "I think between all of us we have $50, tops." "I'll take a check," he says.

"Okay, but I'll make you a wager; after all, you're a gambling club. I'm going to give you a check for $300, take $150 back in chips, and gamble with that."

He said, "What if the check is no good?" "Then the one for $150 won't be good," I pointed out. "Let's go on the assumption that you believe the check will be good. If I lose, the casino gets the other $150, which covers the meal we had yesterday. If I win, I'll pay you what I owe you, and we are even."

The Aviation Club, in Paris
Photo courtesy Club Poker, Paris

He thought about it, smiled and agreed.

He took my check, gave me the $150, and sent two guys to watch me at the baccarat table. Fortunately, I won, ending up with chips worth about $470. I gave the manager the chips and said, "I think you owe me $20."

"Well, you're not going to get it," he said. "That $20 is to pay for my aggravation." He gave me back my check, walked all of us to the door, and quietly said to me, "If I were you, I wouldn't plan on coming back." You can be sure I never did.

The Aviation Club wasn't the end of my gambling on that trip.

A group of us were sitting around, talking about the prices of things in Europe and the United States. I said that, when I was with Lever Brothers, I used to call on drugstores. In Parisian stores, top brands of perfume sold for about a quarter of what they cost in drugstores at home.

I said I didn't have much cash, but if I could borrow some money to buy perfume and bring it back to New York, I could pay it back with 50% interest in 30 days. (At that time you could bring up to $1,000 worth of goods without having to pay tax.)

Two of the people in the group were a guy from Boston and a girl from Seattle, both of whom were studying medicine in France. They decided to "invest" $400 each in my just-hatched perfume venture.

I wrote down their names and addresses, and with their $800 plus a little of my own cash, I bought bottles of Joy and other top-name perfumes. A few days later I went back to New York, and started calling on the same drugstores I used to visit when I was selling Dove soap.

Back then, Joy was unbelievably expensive, about $80 an ounce. Mostly the stores sold quarter- and half-ounce bottles. If the retail price of a bottle was $50, their wholesale cost was close to $40.

I could sell them the same bottle for $30, because I had only paid $15 for it in Paris. The drugstore owner was happy to save money, and I doubled my investment.

It didn't take me long to sell all of the perfume, and I sent each of the medical students $600; their original $400 plus the 50% profit I had promised them. I pocketed about $600, which was about a third of what the entire trip had cost me.

It was only later that I began to think about what led these two people, ordinary students who certainly needed that money, to believe that I could sell the perfume, and that I would keep my promise to repay them.

It showed me that people, even strangers, would come to

trust me very quickly. This seemingly small transaction taught me that others saw me as trustworthy and reliable. That was a very important lesson, and it shaped everything I did in business afterward.

Joy Perfume – my first syndication
Finances Online photo

My Start in Real Estate

With the perfume venture behind me, I had to figure out what I was going to do for a career. One possible path was the securities industry, so I took a test with EF Hutton, then one of the largest stock brokerage firms in the country.

That afternoon, after taking the test, I ran into a Baruch classmate, Al Bronstein. I told him I was starting a training program with Hutton in three weeks, and would go into the securities business when I finished the training.

Al said, "You had thought about real estate. Why don't you do that?" I explained that Hutton would give me a stipend of $500 a month for six months. He said, "You know what, Larry. I have a real estate broker's license. I've been working for my father-in-law, and I'm going to open my own office in the Bronx. Why don't you and I do it together, as partners?"

I told him I didn't have any experience in real estate, but Al was confident we would do well. He said we could at least try it for three weeks, and if I didn't like it I could go with EF Hutton.

It would have cost us $500 to form a corporation to go into business together. We didn't want to spend that, so we took out a yellow pad and wrote out our agreement: "Larry Field and Al Bronstein are partners in a company called A. Bronstein and Company. The business is in the name of Al Bronstein because he's the broker, but we are fifty-fifty partners in all expenses, costs and property."

Al was right. I really enjoyed the real estate business. We sold walk-up apartment houses in the Bronx. Our office was in the back of a storefront insurance company. I made a lot of cold calls, looking for buyers and sellers. I learned a lot from Al, and then picked up a lot about the business myself.

I liked inspecting buildings, going down to the basement and up to the roof. I enjoyed talking to people. That included the tenants, whether it was a commercial or residential building. Does the roof leak? Is the heating good in the winter? Does the landlord maintain the building well? Just commonsense questions.

As I'd found at Lever Brothers, people are happy to talk to you if you really listen to them. Just ask them another question, and after a while they'll tell you anything. I still do this today. If I'm going to buy a retail property, such as a shopping center, I walk into the stores and ask the storekeepers and manager how's it going, how's business, does the owner take care of the building, and so on.

I didn't go to EF Hutton. Al and I did so well that we hired some salesmen. In 1959 we moved to Manhattan, to 507 Fifth Avenue. We had six salesmen plus Al and myself.

About this time I enrolled in law school. Just as happening to meet Al Bronstein led to me going into real estate, bumping into another college buddy resulted in my going to law school.

He and I were at a party, and he said he was about to start at New York Law School (not New York University School of Law, which was a few blocks from my apartment in Greenwich Village.) In fact, he was going to register the next day.

I told him I had been thinking about going to law school. He pointed out that the cost would be covered by the GI Bill. That convinced me, and I went down the next day to meet him — but he didn't show up! He had changed his mind, and never went to law school.

I got accepted by New York Law, and told the school that I'd be using the GI Bill. Three weeks later the registrar called me with bad news. GI Bill benefits had to be used within five years of leaving the military, and according to the U.S. Department of Veteran Affairs, I had applied too late. I had missed the deadline by three or four months.

That meant the end of my plans for law school, because I couldn't afford to pay for tuition, books and fees myself.

The registrar said there was one possible solution, but it was a long shot. I could ask my member of Congress to contact Veterans Affairs and request a waiver of the deadline for me.

John Lindsay, who later became the Mayor of New York, was the congressman for what was called the Silk Stocking District, which included the East Side of Manhattan down to the Village, where Herb Rosenberg and I had an apartment on Fourth Street in what formerly had been the second floor of a bar.

I went to Lindsay's office and met with him. "I'll check on it," he said. "I think we can do it." I told him that if he did, I would always support him. I did get the waiver, and when he ran for mayor I supported him enthusiastically. Herb later also enrolled in law school.

As it turned out, law school for me was a fallback, a way to make a living in case real estate didn't work out. I never practiced law as a profession, but what I learned certainly helped in my business.

A lot of great things happened to me during this period. I met Bill Zeckendorf, the great real estate visionary, just by walking into his office on Madison Avenue. He always was a hero to me because he had the vision and the gumption to do things, all over the country. He developed the Mile High Center in Denver, Place Ville-Marie in Montreal, the Magnificent Mile in Chicago, and Century City in Los Angeles.

He eventually went spectacularly bankrupt, because he wanted to do too much with too little money. The people who really reaped the rewards were the guys who lent him the money, who never would have done what he did because they had no vision.

I was kind of surprised when I got to see him, because I just walked into his office without an appointment. At the end of our talk, when I offered him some property — which was not for him, it was too small — he asked me what I saw going on in the real estate market, what the rents were, what buildings were going for, what I heard on the street.

As I left I thanked him, and admitted I was a little surprised he'd agreed to see me. He said, "I find that people I know, or who work for me, tend to tell me what they think I want to hear. You're telling me what you really think. You don't know I have a half-vacant office building I want to rent. I ask you what rents are going for, and you say they're way down and nobody's going to pay more than four bucks a foot even in the best office building. I'm sitting here with a half-empty building that I need five dollars to break even! Do you think anybody working for me would say what you said?"

That was a very good learning experience. And it was interesting to hear another great real estate figure, Larry Tisch, tell me much the same thing – that unfiltered information is always valuable.

After a year downtown, Al Bronstein decided he was going to become an operator; that is, he would own and manage his own buildings, rather than service other landlords. He went in with his brother and two other partners. He asked me to join them, but I said, "Al, running a business with two people is tough, but your brother-in-law and his two partners and you and me – that would be a disaster." Al and I were together for about three years and did very well, and to this day are very close friends.

He was the one who initially taught me the real estate business, but it was time to move on. Meanwhile, my personal life was changing as well. Not long before, I had met the love of my life.

Eris

Eris and I met in the summer of '59. I had just completed my first year at New York Law. Some guys I knew had rented a house for the summer on Fire Island, a thin spit of land just off the southern coast of Long Island. At the time, groups of young men and women would rent houses on Fire Island from Memorial Day to Labor Day.

You could get there by bridge from Jones Beach, but most people took a ferry from Bay Shore. It was pretty easy to get there from Manhattan. They had a bunch of red wagons that were left at the ferry dock. You could just put your stuff in one and wheel it to the house where you were staying, and bring it back when you left. It was on the honor system.

One of the guys who had rented a house invited me and a friend of ours, Howard Hirschhorn, to come out one weekend in July. We got there late on a Friday afternoon. It was drizzling on Saturday morning, but I decided to go to the beach. This was going to be my only weekend off, because I would be taking law school classes for the rest of the summer.

I put on my bathing suit, took a towel, and went downstairs, where the guys from the house and a bunch of girls from another house were playing records and talking. I asked if anyone wanted to join me at the beach, and they looked at me like I was nuts.

An hour later I was back from my swim, changed my clothes and joined the group. I looked around and saw this very attractive, slim, dark-haired girl with a great figure. I was really intrigued, and had to talk to her. She told me her name was Eris. I'd never heard of a name like that. We talked a lot that afternoon. I invited her to have dinner with me, and she accepted.

She was in the same position as I was. Some girlfriends of hers had rented a house, and one of them invited Eris and her friend and roommate, Shelly Pradell, to visit for the weekend. After dinner we walked around Ocean Bay Park and went to parties, which is what everybody did. You went to houses of other people, and brought your own drinks and a bag of potato chips. That was the party. I had a wonderful time.

I walked Eris back to her house, and sort of hinted that I wouldn't mind spending the night there. She pointed out that she was sharing a bedroom with two other girls, so I went back to "my" house, where I slept on an air mattress on the floor.

The next day, Sunday, we met for breakfast, spent the morning together, and then lunch. Howard and I had a car, so I suggested that we drive Eris and Shelly back to Manhattan. They lived on 34th Street and I was on Fourth Street, not far by car. Eris and I made a date for dinner and drinks the next evening.

I was smitten. I liked her intelligence, her bearing, her attractiveness, the way she spoke, and especially the way she would stick up for her ideas. I feel the best relationship is when you're equals; if one person is always dominant, it doesn't work.

What did she see in me? I think she liked my honesty and openness. I think she appreciated the way I treated her, not casually but with great respect.

She knew my feelings, because I made it clear very quickly that I really wanted to see her all the time.

Later she told me she also thought that I would be successful, although neither of us ever dreamed of the real success we would enjoy, or could conceive of how our lives would eventually turn out. We used to talk about someday making a million dollars, but that was just a figure of speech, an unreachable goal that gave you something to strive for.

And as far as what Eris saw in me, I should also point out that the Larry Field of 1959 was much thinner and better looking.

From the time I first met her, I fell really hard. By the second or third date I knew this was a serious romance, that I really, really liked this person.

I use the word "like," because in a marriage you've got to like somebody as well as love them. Loving is one thing and liking is something else.

I can only tell you that within six or eight weeks, when Eris told me she was leaving for California, I could not bear to lose her, and I asked her to marry me. More about that soon.

At that time I was going to law school and working as an independent broker, so I usually wore a suit or jacket and tie, and carried an attaché case. On one of our first dates back in the city, I showed up at Eris' apartment and she clearly was

Eris, in 1959

impressed by how I looked.

I put my attaché case on the coffee table and opened it up. Inside, instead of important documents, was a bottle of wine and some cheese. She and Shelly had a good laugh.

Eris was working for a man named Jack Einiger, who had a company called Einiger Mills, which manufactured and sold wool and cashmere fabrics. He was a terrific guy, very successful and generous; he was a founder of the Albert Einstein College of Medicine at Yeshiva University.

He treated his staff the way I now treat mine. Eris was his secretary-assistant and did everything for him, from making his appointments to picking out his Christmas gifts. They had a company station wagon, for small deliveries, and a company apartment where Jack could stay if he had to be in the city late.

Jack let Eris use the station wagon and apartment on the weekends. Thanks to him, from Friday night through Monday morning we had all the liquor we wanted, which wasn't much because neither of us drank much, and I learned how to smoke Jack's very good cigars. It was sort of like Eris came with a dowry!

We went out almost every night, and talked all the time. I learned that she was born in Brooklyn and grew up there until she was about 15 years old, when her family moved to Los Angeles. She went to Fairfax High School, and then to UCLA for a couple of semesters.

Then she stunned me with the news that she would be going back to California in October. She was homesick. She had a big family in Los Angeles, and she missed them. "It's time to go back," she said. We had just met in July, and I knew I could not lose her.

I said, "If we got married, would you reconsider going back to Los Angeles?" "Yeah, I would." "Well, I'd like to marry you." We went to a little jewelry shop in the Village and had a ring designed. It was actually two rings, one a wedding band and the other with a diamond, that fit together or could be worn separately. I think they cost about $300, which was a lot of money then.

After one of our dates, Eris and I came to my place, the apartment that was converted from the upper floor of a speakeasy. We were sitting by the fireplace in the front room, and I had to go to the bathroom. I heard Eris let out a yell, and came running back. Eris was standing in the middle of the room, staring at the fire escape door. A guy was coming in, carrying bongo drums. People knew the fire door was always open, and they used it as a shortcut to the street from the alley behind the building, walking through my apartment and out the front door.

It took Eris a while to get used to my oddball Greenwich Village neighbors. Once, while I was out of the apartment, some friends were sitting around, drinking a little too much. My furniture was mostly odds and ends, including some coffee tables made from wood cable spools and milk crates.

They decided to start a fire in the fireplace, and used my tables as fuel. I got more spools and kegs to "re-furnish" my apartment, but Eris laid down the law: "This kind of thing is not going to happen after we are married." And it didn't.

We found an apartment on Morton Street, and set the wedding date for January 31, 1960, a Sunday. It was between sessions at law school, so I was off for a couple of weeks.

It's a wonderful feeling to find somebody who you want to be with for the rest of your life. We went to little restaurants and coffee shops on Bleecker Street, saw offbeat young comedians like Woody Allen, Lenny Bruce and Mort Sahl, went to the theater and museums, and really explored New York.

I didn't meet Eris' parents, Irwin and Rose Perll, until they came to New York just before the wedding. Irwin was a real character. He was the only house painter I ever heard of who didn't have a car or truck. When he painted houses in Los Angeles, he took a bus, with his ladder, tarps and paint cans.

He was the opposite of everybody else in the family. They were all liberal Democrats, he was a conservative Republican. They all rooted for the Dodgers, because the whole family came from Brooklyn, but he was a Giants fan. He was definitely different, a little curmudgeonly, but a very gentle person.

Her mother came from a family of six daughters and two brothers. Five of the sisters – Rose, Pearl, Mildred, Lillian, and Helen – had moved to Los Angeles right after World War II, while her sister Sally and her brothers Phil and Lou, and others in the Miller family, stayed in Brooklyn. One sister had moved to Los Angeles because her husband had been in California during military service and liked it so much that they decided to move here.

Little by little, as often happens, other siblings decided to join them. The two brothers were salesmen, one in the paper business and the other one in textiles. The brothers-in-law all worked with their hands, as craftsmen. One was a carpenter, one was a refrigeration repairman, one was in the egg business. Their children were first generation college people, like Eris and me.

As I discovered, I was entering into a very close, loving family.

I'll never forget when Eris' parents came to New York and met my mother and father. Irwin was born on New York's Lower East Side. His family had come from Poland, and Rose had been born in Poland and came here as a young girl with her parents. Her younger siblings were born in the United States.

We all went to Luchow's, a famous old restaurant on 14th Street in the East Village. My father, whose first job in America had been as a waiter, kept jumping up to get us water or bread, instead of asking the waiter.

My mother, who didn't know how to talk to people, was almost silent, except when she was shown some photos of Eris' family. She blurted out an awkward comment about a short sister marrying a tall man and a tall sister marrying a shorter man.

Irwin, whose nickname was ltchy, was on his best behavior, probably after receiving a lecture from Rose and Eris.

It was a long, awkward lunch.

Eris and I planned the wedding and paid for it. Neither of our parents could afford to do that, and we certainly didn't want to strain their resources.

As it happened, Eris' cousins, Bob and Ruth Blair, were moving to a new house in Roslyn, Long Island, early in January. Ruth very generously offered us the use of their home for the wedding. We'd just have to rent some chairs, because they didn't have much furniture – but that meant there was more room for guests.

Herb Rosenberg, my roommate in the Village, was my best man, and my friends Mort Gerberg and Howard Hirschhorn were there. In all we probably had 60 to 80 people. A rabbi from a local temple officiated.

My mother arrived late. When I asked her why, she said, "Oh, I have such a headache I almost didn't come at all." Only my mother would consider not attending her son's wedding because of a headache.

Other than my mother's late arrival, there were no incidents. Nobody got drunk. It was family and a bunch of friends, and everyone got along. We had a little orchestra, which played nicely. We had a cousin of mine take pictures, which were just terrible. We wound up with only one picture of Eris and me at the wedding. It taught me to use a professional photographer,

Our wedding photo - the only one that came out

not a friend or a relative.

But the wedding was perfect where it really counted, because Eris and I had nearly half a century together in which we built a happy, loving life, highlighted by two wonderful children, two delightful grandchildren, a fantastic son-in-law, business success, and the opportunity to share our good fortune with others.

Our apartment on Morton Street was tiny; the whole place was probably smaller than my office. When you walked in the front door there was a small living room, the kitchen, a bathroom, and a bedroom so small we had to climb over the bed to get to the dresser. We loved it.

Eris painted the whole apartment, including the furniture, and we somehow managed to host parties with three to five other couples in that little place. You don't need a mansion to have fun, and for us it was a very happy time.

The apartment was on the fourth floor of a five-story walkup. When Eris became pregnant, it was clear that schlepping a baby carriage and groceries up those stairs was not going to work. We moved to Queens, where our first daughter, Lisa, was born on February 10, 1961. (Within a few days of Lisa's arrival, I changed from day to evening classes at law school.)

Our new apartment was on 68th Avenue, in Forest Hills. It was a modest rental building, but it had a doorman and a garage. Why? Because one of the tenants was Harry LeFrak, the father of Sam LeFrak, one of the biggest real estate developers in the country.

The LeFrak group built more than 200,000 apartments in and around New York, including Battery Park City and LeFrak City. Needless to say, the building was very well maintained, which was very nice for us and the other tenants.

I was 29 when we got married, which was a little older than average for men at that time. You never know when or where you are going to find that person who is right for you. But I think being a little older is a help, because you know yourself better.

Both Eris and I were more mature than a lot of our friends. We'd both had a taste of success. I hadn't had great financial success yet, but at least I was on a path in real estate. Eris had held a very responsible position in a successful company.

People often asked us how Eris got her name. Her mother, Rose, had two miscarriages before she became pregnant with Eris. Her parents were so nervous about the risk of another miscarriage that they didn't pick a name, so after Eris was born Rose looked through a book of baby names and picked "Eris" – even though the book said it was the name of the Greek goddess of discord. Rose wanted a name beginning with an E, and didn't like Edith, Ethel or other common names. She loved the name Eris.

Although most of her family was on the West Coast, Eris did have some aunts, uncles and cousins in New York. Her Aunt Sally was married to Jack Blaustein, who was in the wig business. They had three sons and a daughter: Bob, who was in the apparel business, Lanny, who joined the wig business, Richie, who was in the toy business, and Bonnie, who was a secretary in a brokerage house.

Richie was a very warm, funny man who had an apartment in the same building where we lived in Queens, on the same floor. He would often babysit for Lisa, and on nights I came home early from school, the three of us would play cards. It was always the two of them against me, because I'd say something obnoxious like, "You guys can't beat me," just to tease them. It was great having Richie nearby, because he and Eris were so close.

My mother and father were no help whatsoever. My mother probably resented the fact that Eris had taken away her son, even though I had left both physically and in spirit years before. She couldn't let go.

Here's an example, from shortly before Eris and I got married. My parents had moved to an apartment on Williams Bridge Road, near the Einstein Hospital. My mother's cousin, a Holocaust survivor, had a daughter who was engaged to a doctor who was doing his residency at Einstein. The cousin asked if her daughter could stay at my parents' house on a few weekends when she was visiting her fiancée.

My mother told her, "Well, I'll have to find out when Larry is going to be here." I hadn't lived with them for four years, and I had started on a new life with Eris, but my mother couldn't let go. And it would drive me nuts.

Her behavior got to Eris as well. When we went there for dinner, my mother would cook enormous amounts of food, then stand over us and say, "Eat some more." This was after you've already eaten for two people, and can't eat any more. When we left, she insisted that we take enough leftovers for at least two or three more meals.

Eris tried to politely decline the leftovers, explaining that with me in school most evenings, we don't eat much at home, and the food would go to waste. My mother ignored her, and kept sending us home with leftovers. Soon Eris was seething; this was not about food, it was about who was going to win.

One evening, as we were driving back from the Bronx to Manhattan, she and I got into a huge fight about the food. We were on the West Side Highway, near the Hudson River. I stopped the car, took the food and threw it toward the river.

Later, I realized I had behaved like an idiot, and the next time we had dinner at my parents' place I told my mother she could wrap up the leftovers if she wanted to, but we were not going to take them, so she'd have to give them to somebody else.

After this, Eris always talked about my "Hungarian temper." I can only think of one other time when I really blew my top. It was the biggest fight we ever had, and I am not sure what it was about – although chances are pretty good it involved something my mother had done.

I got so upset that I grabbed a very fancy carving set that we had received as a wedding gift and threw it down the incinerator.

For those who didn't grow up in a New York apartment building, the incinerator was a shaft in the hallway into which the tenants threw their garbage. It fell to the basement, where it was fed into a furnace and burned.

That was the end of the carving set, but it was better than getting violent.

Law School and Working For Ron Platt

I finished law school in 1963; it took me an extra year because I had switched to evening classes. Early on I had worked with Al Bronstein, selling apartment buildings. When Al decided he wanted to be an owner rather than a sales agent, which wasn't for me, we had parted as friends.

Then, early in 1960, I joined a syndicator named Ron Platt. (A syndicator brings in a group of investors to purchase and jointly own a property.) In my entire career, this was my only salaried job in real estate.

Ron Platt was a very unusual guy. He lived with a male psychiatrist at a time when gay people were forced to be secretive about their sexual orientation. He was one of the best people I've ever known at marketing. He knew very little about real estate, but he felt he didn't have to, because he believed that what people buy is the person doing the selling.

He was far better at raising money than buying properties or managing them. That was the part he had problems with. I had a title of vice president, but as was usual with Ron there was no specific job description for my role. But I was the only person there who knew anything about real estate, so my job was to oversee the management of all the properties the company was syndicating.

At different times there were eight, ten or twelve properties, in different parts of the country. My job was to go out and evaluate new purchases. I did, but Ron really didn't listen. He felt that, if it looked good in the prospectus and he wrote it up well, he'd get the money from investors. In fact, that's what happened.

To this day, I am always cautious when people send me great looking prospectuses with beautiful pictures and descriptions, elaborately printed and bound. In my view, the fancier the cover and the writing, the less merit it probably has.

I handled everything that had to do with evaluating and purchasing the real estate. I would give my report to Ron, but he made the final decisions. It was a small operation. In addition to me, he just had a couple of bookkeepers and secretaries. He used local real estate managers in the different cities to handle the day-to-day operations of the properties, and I would oversee their work.

It was a great job for me, because after being just a real estate broker, this gave me the feeling of what it was like to be an owner. Ron Platt, his company and the investors were the actual owners, but I was making all the decisions that an owner would normally make. Ron didn't want to get involved with things like whether to re-carpet the hallways, upgrade the electricity or replace the air conditioning system.

Ron was very eclectic. He bought everything, from motels to offices to shops and stores. We had office buildings in Albany and Rochester, and I'd fly up to one or the other every week. I had carte blanche in running this diverse portfolio of properties, which was a great learning experience.

I was paid about $80,000 a year, an immense salary for that time. Ron was very generous with everybody in the office. There were even bonuses. One year I made $100,000. (When I finished law school in 1963, I looked at what law firms were paying. The salaries were about $2,000 a month, when I was making $7,000 or $8,000 a month.)

Ron knew he was paying above-market salaries, but he felt by doing so he would get the best possible work from his people, because they didn't want to lose their job. I would have worked just as hard for a lower salary, but I follow Ron's example today, and pay above the market with the salaries of the people in my office.

As a result, we have very competent people, and they stay with us. Without them, and the high quality of their work, I wouldn't have this business. One person can't do it. Someone who worries about whether an employee should earn $20 more or less per week is not going to be a big success.

My philosophy is that you should share your success, and the more you share, the more you get. With all his flaws, Ron taught me that.

Eris and I on vacation in the 1960s

From observing Ron I also learned that, while it's important to be good at marketing, you still have to have a product that earns some money, and you have to manage it well. Similarly, watching Ron taught me not to be so taken with people that you lose your good judgment.

Possibly because of his own insecurities, Ron would unquestioningly accept whatever was said by people who were selling him something, especially if they were well-known or seemed to be successful.

This became apparent when I checked on two hotels that he

was planning to purchase from a couple of smooth guys who bought, managed and sold hotels. Ron had the properties under contract when I joined the company, and he told me to go look at them. One was in Palo Alto, south of San Francisco, and the other was in Georgetown, next to Washington, D.C. I had never done anything with hotels, and didn't know much about them, but I figured it's real estate, so I could figure it out.

The hotel in Palo Alto was in a great location. It was across the street from one of the best hotels in the city. Our rooms were cheaper, so I figured we should at least get some of the overflow. I had dinner at the hotel, a steak, and it was not very good. I went back to the kitchen.

The chef was not there, so I talked to the cook about the steak. His answer was simple: "It's what the chef buys." I did some digging, and discovered that the chef would order prime cuts of meat, but the vendor would send lower-quality cuts, bill the hotel for the better meat, and give the chef a kickback.

I uncovered a similar scheme at the Georgetown hotel. The grosses were very different from what the seller had told us they would be. Either they had inflated the numbers, or something had gone very wrong.

Looking over the books, I noticed that one day we paid a laundry service for 70 sets of sheets, but the ledger showed only 50 rooms had been occupied.

A little after midnight, when nothing was going on, I started chatting with the night clerk. I asked him about the discrepancy between the room count and the laundry. At first he dodged the issue, but when I asked him directly if some of the room rentals were not going into the books, he admitted they were. He had worked at the hotel for five years.

A new manager had taken over about 18 months ago, who brought in a new bookkeeper, a woman, and they just happened to live together. Their cozy relationship made it easy for them to hide some room rentals every day, and pocket the money.

Discovering these kinds of problems is easy. If you look carefully and ask some questions, you will generally find out what's going on. The meat purveyor giving a kickback to the chef quickly gave me the details, because he was really uncomfortable with the arrangement.

Most people aren't dishonest. They hate it when others cheat, they don't want to be part of it, and they don't want to be seen as thieves.

I gave Ron a written report detailing what was going on at the two hotels. I said I thought they were bad deals, and we should pull out of the purchase contracts. A week went by, with no word from Ron. I finally asked him what he thought.

He said he had sent the sellers my report. Then he asked them to come in, and in essence they called me a liar. "We don't know why Larry would say something like that," they said. "Maybe he doesn't like us."

I didn't get mad. I just said, "What reason would I have to do that? Do you think I made up these numbers?" In the end, Ron said to them, "Maybe Larry was overzealous. I think that we can complete this transaction."

He bought both hotels, and of course lost millions. But it was not his money. It was investors' money.

Ron was not a crook. He didn't steal anybody's money, but he dissipated it. He could write prospectuses and raise money, but he didn't know how to run a property the way it should be run. He believed his own excessively optimistic promises. Yet he was basically a nice guy, and to the day he died I really liked him. But he ran his company into the ground, and he was forced out in 1962.

New people took over, and bought out his investors for 50 cents on the dollar. They kept me around for four months, to get all the information they needed from me, and then of course I was fired.

My experience working with Ron taught me a lot about how to treat investors' money – which is the opposite of how Ron operated. I knew that I would have to raise capital from other people to buy property, because I didn't have that kind of money myself.

I decided that I would treat the money I raised from investors better than I treated my own. I would be much more careful with their money than with mine.

Ron's downfall reinforced my belief that you have to treat investors' money very, very responsibly, because doing otherwise – whether you steal it or are simply inept – will ruin your reputation. It was clear to me that character, integrity and reputation are the best assets you can have in business, and in life.

Looking back, a great many of the things I've done in my life, even the negative experiences, have turned out in some way to be helpful or useful to me. In the Army I trained to be a Ranger, until pneumonia and then a paperwork snafu turned me into a teacher. In Europe, the Aviation Club showed me that there is no free lunch, while my little perfume venture was my introduction to syndication, and to what you can accomplish when others trust you. At Lever Brothers I learned I could sell – and that I didn't want to climb the corporate ladder.

I started in real estate with my friend and partner Al Bronstein, only to have to leave that partnership when our goals diverged – but leave with valuable knowledge of real estate. I was fired after Ron Platt's company imploded, but took with me a hands-on experience in real estate management and a deeper appreciation of the obligations owed to investors who provide the capital that makes our projects possible.

Later, when I went to other people to raise money for real estate projects, I never promised more than I knew I could deliver. In Paris, when I told the two medical students that I could give them a 50% return on their money by reselling perfume, I knew I could do it. If worse came to worst, I could take less profit for myself, or just break even, but I could at least give them what I had promised.

To me it's vitally important to maintain your good name, to have integrity and be honest and straightforward. If you lie or cheat, you will suffer the consequences. You may not go to jail, but others will hear about what you did, and they're not going to invest with you. Because of the way I've run my life, people want to be my partner.

As a matter of fact, the perception of my success is such that years ago we stopped bidding on properties in my name. Instead, we buy in the name of a corporation. Too often the seller would say, "Oh, Larry's interested, so it's got to be worth more," or other buyers would figure it had to be a worthwhile property and would try to outbid us. That's what happens when you have a reputation for being knowledgeable and above-board.

I'm proud of how we do business and what we have accomplished for ourselves and our investors, but I don't regard our properties as monuments to our success. In my heart I know that we are really only caretakers of whatever we own. We have it for the period of time that we're around, and then it's in the hands of someone else.

I've also come to see that pursuing wealth for its own sake isn't very rewarding. After you've reached a certain level, accumulating more money has little meaning. Money doesn't buy health, or happiness, the love of your children or the respect of your friends. It just buys material things. They are nice, even great to have, and I'm all for them. And money gives you the ability to support good causes, as I've had the great pleasure to do. But money can't buy you what I think are the most important things: peace of mind and well-being.

Doing some real estate business outdoors

There's something else that made my life easier. I never felt I had to impress my parents with my accomplishments. They made it clear they loved me unconditionally and felt that whatever I did was wonderful. What it was didn't matter. My father would always say, in his Hungarian accent, "Everybody loves Larry."

When I told my dad I was making $80,000 a year, it was hard

for him to comprehend that amount, because I don't think he ever made more than about $10,000 per year. The amount I was being paid was amazing to them. But they mostly were concerned that I was okay. They had been very worried when I left Lever Brothers, a big company where I got a steady paycheck, and instead was working with Al for an unpredictable commission.

The fact that I got a salary when I worked with Ron was more important to them than the immense amount I was receiving. The money didn't make them think more of me. I could have been a teacher or worked for the post office; it wouldn't have mattered.

Although I had been fired from what had been Ron's company, I was on a pretty solid financial footing because of the very generous salary I had received. Now I had to look around for what I wanted to do next.

It was 1963, and the New York World's Fair was coming to Flushing, Queens, not far from where I lived. Everyone was excited about the Fair, but I had no idea that it would be another important turning point in my career.

Renting Apartments

The city was changing the zoning in some parts of Queens in 1963, reducing the number of apartments you could build on a piece of land. Instead of 100 apartments in a six-story building, you would only be allowed to have 50. The rule would take effect in two years. As a result, developers were racing to construct six-story, 100-apartment buildings before the new rule took effect.

With all those new buildings coming onto the market, there were loads of vacant apartments.

I decided to become a rental agent, finding tenants for those apartments in return for commissions from the landlords. I started by walking into buildings in the neighborhood, finding out how many vacancies there were, and getting the name of the owner. Then I called the owners and asked to see them because I could rent out their empty apartments.

The first two I spoke to were real estate professionals, and they had no interest in engaging me. Not a great start.

At the third building, a pretty large one, I was told to see the owner's accountant. When I got to the accountant's office,

I asked to talk to the building owner. The accountant wanted to know why. "Well, I was at his building, and I noticed that there's about 200 apartments, and the superintendent told me only 22 are occupied. At that rate he's going to lose the building or need a lot of money to carry a big loan."

The accountant said, "Well, that's true... and you think you can rent them?" "I know I can." "Okay."

We walked to the back of the accountant's office, and I saw a man who was literally hiding there. Why? Because about 100 people had invested anywhere from $5,000 to $20,000 with him to build his apartment building. (At the time, the average annual income for a family in New York was about $4,500, so these were pretty significant investments.) He was about to lose it all, and was terrified of what they would do to him.

He was a furrier, and he wasn't even doing well as a furrier. He had no background in real estate, but he had syndicated this property to all his friends. Now he's hiding out in his accountant's office, because the bank was threatening to foreclose on the property, which meant he and his syndicate partners would lose everything.

I gave him my pitch. I said, "Look, I think I can rent your apartments. I'm going to charge you two months' rent. You don't pay me until your tenants pay their rent. I'll collect the rent, deposit it and take my money from that deposit."

He said, "I have no money for ads." "All right, I'll pay for the ads, and if I have to employ other people, I'll pay for that too."

"It won't cost me anything?" "No, it won't. And I'm telling you that within six months you'll have at least another 50 to 75 apartments rented, and people living there."

I had no idea if I would be able to do this. But he was desperate, it wouldn't cost him anything, and I looked and acted very confident. He figured he might as well give me a chance, and we signed a contract.

I ran an ad the next weekend, and was at the building to see prospective tenants on Saturday, Sunday and all of the following week. Then I visited the superintendent. (For non-New Yorkers, a building superintendent, or "super," handles maintenance and minor repairs in apartment buildings for the landlord, often getting a free or discounted apartment as well as a salary.)

I told the super I'd be running another ad the following weekend, and would be there on Saturday and Sunday, but not during the week. I'd leave a sign on the entrance, "See Superintendent About Rentals." If someone showed up Monday through Friday, he was to show them the apartments and take their name, address and phone number.

I'd give the super $5 for each one, even if they didn't rent an apartment. If they did, I'd give him another $25. That was nice money at the time, for not much work. Most of the people came on the weekends, but a handful did come during the week, so he was happy.

Pretty soon it got so busy that I realized I couldn't handle it by myself on the weekends. To this day I don't know if it was the ads that brought them in, or if it was just good timing – that more people happened to be looking for apartments.

I hired a couple of friends to help on the weekends. I told them I'd pay them $50 for each apartment they rented.

A typical six-story Bronx apartment building
New York City Municipal Archives photo

To keep them from fighting over the commissions, I told them they'd split the total; if one guy rented three apartments and the other guy did five, that's eight apartments at $50, or $400, so they'd each get $200. If I rented an apartment while they were there, they'd also get $50 on the one I rented.

By the fourth week I was only coming by at the busiest times. The guys were happy to pick up their money, and the super was overjoyed.

Then the furrier came by … and went to work for me, renting apartments in his own building to get the $50!

Banzai!

About the sixth week we were there, one of the guys came to me and said, "There's a Japanese guy here who says he may need four or six apartments, furnished." The man told me he had been hired by the Japanese government. Japan would be exhibiting at the World's Fair, and they wanted him to rent apartments for their staff.

I asked for details about what they needed, but he didn't know. He'd have to get the information and come back. I said, "Why don't you tell me who you're talking to. I'll give you 5% of whatever I do with them. You don't have to worry about coming and going, or being an intermediary."

He agreed, and introduced me to the people who were in charge of the Japanese pavilion. The Chief Financial Officer was a young guy about my age, who had studied here and spoke perfect English. The president of the organization was the former head of Japanese TV, who looked like an admiral in a movie, with a bullet head and no hair. He didn't speak English.

It took a long time to get information from them. They kept saying they weren't sure what they needed. Meanwhile, I continued running ads and scrounging for tenants.

Eventually the Japanese group said they might need 50 apartments. Good, we had 50. "We want them furnished." Okay, I'll buy the furniture and add the cost to the rent, divided by 24 because they wanted a two-year lease. At the end of the lease they could keep the furniture, or the building's owner would dump it.

"Okay, well, maybe we need 100 apartments now." That could be a problem. By now, six months had gone by, and the ads were really working. Every weekend we were renting four to eight apartments. There were maybe 100 left now, and soon there would be less. Then I thought, maybe I'll make a deal with owners of other apartment buildings.

I was meeting with the Japanese at least twice a month. At one meeting, they said they now thought they needed 200 apartments. Each would have four girls working as hostesses at their pavilion, plus an older woman as a chaperone. And they only wanted the apartments for the months the Fair was open. The Fair would close in November of 1964 and reopen in March of 1965.

As if this wasn't complicated enough, the guy in charge said, through his interpreter, "Maybe it would be cheaper for us to just buy a building, and sell it later." I had no idea if that was true, and said so. He said, "You prepare a report for us, giving us the pros and cons of renting or buying."

I did the report, analyzing their options very carefully, and I came to the conclusion that it was not a good idea for the Japanese government to own apartments.

They would have to buy a whole building, and when the Fair was over they'd be left with an empty building full of used furniture. They'd have to employ a superintendent, which meant paying Social Security, they'd have to have liability insurance, and if there were tenants in the building who were not from the Japanese pavilion, they'd have obligations to them.

I gave them a report that said it would be cheaper and easier for them to rent the apartments they needed, and the furniture, and be done with everything when the Fair was over.

Meanwhile, I was talking to other building owners about finding tenants for their apartments. One guy says to me, "Who are you wanting to rent these 50 apartments for?" I told him it was for the staff of the Japanese pavilion for the World's Fair. He looked at me and said, "I can deal with them directly. Why do I need you?"

I told him he probably could, but that wouldn't be ethical. After all, I was doing all the work. He didn't seem impressed by my argument.

The schedule was getting tight, and I kept telling the Japanese executives that they had to act soon if they wanted to have the apartments they needed by the opening of the Fair in April of 1964.

The 1964 World's Fair

Alamy, Ltd. photo

They called me in to a meeting in their office, which was set up like offices in Japan. The assistants were all in an open area; only the president and the CFO had private offices.

When we met, we always had tea at a round table in an open area, where young women in kimonos would serve us, never in one of the private offices. I asked the CFO why, and he explained that, to the Japanese, meeting with a guest in an office, across a desk, is considered impolite, because it implies the executive is in a position of power. Sitting at a round table, with everyone in the same kind of chair, made everyone equal.

It had been weeks since I submitted my report. When we sat down, the CFO said, "We asked somebody else to do a report, just to check on yours." He showed it to me, and of course it had been written by the building owner I had contacted about renting more apartments.

He not only had gone behind my back to contact the Japanese directly, but he'd swiped entire paragraphs from my report, which obviously they had let him review. Not surprisingly, he'd come to the same conclusion I had. I was furious, but something told me to wait and see what happened.

I looked at it, I said, "I'm glad you got a second opinion, and that the two reports agree." I put it back on the table.

The President, the bullet-headed guy who looked like central casting's idea of a Japanese admiral, was almost always silent at our meetings. This time he reached for the other guy's report, ripped it in half, and dropped it on the table. Then he said, in English, "But we trust you."

The CFO said, "We need 200 apartments." That was it. We never had a written contract, and never used a lawyer.

In the end I leased 220 apartments for them in six buildings. I asked for a check for $100,000 for the furniture. They handed it to me, still without a formal agreement. "Oh no, we trust you, you take care of it."

When the Fair opened, Eris and I were invited to the opening of the Japanese pavilion. We sat through a lot of speeches in Japanese, having no idea what it was about.

I was holding a drink when suddenly everyone was shouting, "Banzai! Banzai!" That sure got my attention, because I knew that was a Japanese battle cry in World War II. I learned it is also used to express enthusiasm or support; it means "may you live 10,000 years!"

I certainly was enthusiastic about our relationship, in part because we had become very friendly over all these months, and because I had made about $100,000 from their leases in a period of a year, on top of the money I made renting apartments to all the people who were brought in by the ads I ran.

Leasing out the apartments was a huge success, from a standing start. It confirmed my belief that I would do better on my own. Yes, it sometimes feels like you are skating on thin ice, because there's nobody to write a check if things go wrong. But it was exciting, almost an adventure, and I met a lot of very interesting people.

I knew I would never go back to working for someone else.

That doesn't mean it was all fun. The mama-sans, the chaperones for the Japanese Pavilion hostesses, would never call the live-in superintendent of the building when something was wrong. If a toilet clogged, they called Larry.

I'd get home and Eris would give me a big smile and pass along a message about the stuffed toilet in such-and-such apartment. It might be 10:00 at night, but I'd call the super and get it fixed.

The next day I'd remind the woman who had reported the problem and remind her that she could just call the superintendent herself. I'd given each of them a list of the names and phone numbers to call.

The next time there was a problem, she'd call me. It was part of my continuing education in the real estate business.

A view of the Fair, showing the roof of the Japanese Pavilion
David McBride Photo

Eris' Sudden Illness and the Move West

In the Fall of 1964, Eris had a sore throat that wouldn't go away. We went to our local doctor in Queens, who gave her penicillin. A couple of weeks later she still wasn't better. Then her back bothered her; she had chronic problems from a disc. We decided to go to an osteopath, who was sort of a cross between a medical doctor and a chiropractor.

Before he did any manipulation for her back problem, he did a physical exam. He looked in her mouth with a tongue depressor, and told her she had to see a physician, because something was pushing one of her tonsils out of place.

Rather than going back to our family doctor, we decided she should see Arthur Mankiewicz, the brother-in-law of Al Bronstein, my friend and former business partner. Dr. Mankiewicz was a Park Avenue doctor and a wonderful diagnostician, whom we had seen a few times when we lived in Manhattan.

Eris thought it was silly to see him for just a cold, but we went.

We told him what the osteopath had seen. After he examined Eris, he said she should go to an ear, nose and throat specialist, and recommended one.

That doctor lanced the swelling, but when we went back to see Arthur a few days later, it hadn't improved. He said we should go back to the specialist and have her tonsils removed.

I went with Eris to the hospital. They told us tonsillectomies usually took only 20 to 30 minutes, and took her into the operating room.

After about 10 minutes the doctor came out and told me that, after they had put her under anesthesia, they found a very large growth in her throat. He said it would have to be removed by a specialist. When Eris woke up, we went home.

We went back to Arthur, who sent us to a friend of his who was the head surgeon at the Sloan Kettering Institute, which at that time was one of the leading hospitals in cancer surgery. It is still a major cancer research center.

I think the doctor's name was Gazelle, but am not sure. He examined her, and said he didn't think it was very serious. He scheduled her for what he called a "radical tonsillectomy" a week later, at 8 a.m., and told his secretary to book another patient that day at 11 a.m. The secretary then told us, apologetically, that their minimum charge for an operation was $500, even though the usual charge for a tonsillectomy at the time was $75 to $100.

A week later Eris checked into the hospital, and just before 8 a.m. was taken to the operating room. I waited. Nine o'clock passed, then ten o'clock, eleven, twelve. I was getting antsy.

I called the surgeon's office, but his secretary had no information. She said Dr. Gazelle was probably doing the other operation and just hadn't had a chance to come out and see me.

I wanted to believe that. After the examination he had been so reassuring that I couldn't imagine it was something too serious. I always go on the assumption that things will be okay.

By two o'clock I was getting very anxious. It was after 2:30 when he finally came in. I was only anxious because of the delay; it never occurred to me that there might be something seriously wrong. He was the leading head-and-neck surgeon in New York, maybe even the United States, and he had told us it would be a radical tonsillectomy. That didn't sound like a big deal to me. I thought the delay had been because of the next patient.

The growth in Eris' throat was malignant, Dr. Gazelle said, "It turned out to be far more extensive than I thought." The growth was the size of a small lemon. It was fortunate that it had pushed against the tonsil, because that made it visible.

It was so large that he couldn't take it out through her mouth. He had to cut into her neck and remove it through that opening. The growth went back behind her ear, and they had to proceed very carefully because of all the nerves and muscles in that area of her head.

Eris was very uncomfortable, with a breathing tube down her throat. When he took it out the next day, Eris and I asked about her prognosis, and what would happen if the tumor came back. He said, "We went as far as we could. It looked very clean to me."

However, he said, if the tumor returned it would be very, very difficult to do more surgery. The malignancy would probably spread to her brain, and she would not survive.

After he left, Eris and I talked for a long time. Eris had already been dealing with a lot.

Her mother had passed away a few months earlier, followed by her father about six weeks later. Irwin died of a heart attack, although he had no history of heart trouble. It

Eris with Lisa in a stroller, 1963

seemed he just didn't want to live without Rose. They needed each other, and he especially needed her.

Lisa was now about three and a half years old. Robyn had

been born in March of 1964, when Eris was feeling sick from what turned out to be the tumor.

We now had two children to think about, including what we would do if the cancer did come back. We felt it would be better to be in Los Angeles if that happened, where Eris had a large and close family, including a sister, numerous aunts and uncles and cousins, as well as many friends.

By January of 1965, we had decided to move to Los Angeles.

We knew it was the right decision, but Eris was very concerned about my work, because I was doing well in New York.

Of course, it turned out that I became very successful here, and we thrived in Los Angeles. Our family has enjoyed a very fortunate life, with a wonderful circle of friends, and I have loved living and working here.

This reinforces my belief that everything that happens in your life – even if it looks bad at the moment – opens a door to something that can be positive. Because of Eris' very frightening medical problem, we came to Los Angeles.

I have often thought about what would have happened if Eris hadn't gotten sick. There's no doubt in my mind that we would have stayed in New York. I had just had the success with the Japanese government during the World's Fair, and am confident I could have built on that and been as successful in New York, and perhaps more, because there the numbers are bigger.

But life in New York is different from Los Angeles. Even for the wealthiest people in Manhattan, everyday life is still a challenge. It's not easy to get around the city. Even if you have a chauffeur, it still takes half an hour just to go across Manhattan.

So, even though the reason for our move was our deep concern about what Eris' situation might mean for her and our family, ultimately everything worked out for the best. California has been wonderful for us, personally and professionally, and that's where our story heads next.

California, Here We Come!

We moved to Los Angeles in June of 1965. We stayed with Eris' sister Roberta, who everybody called Bobbie, and her husband, Harvey Goldberg, who generously put us up in their very small house. Our furniture arrived about two and a half weeks later.

By then we had found a house on La Jolla Avenue, just south of Olympic Boulevard, in the Carthay Circle District. It was a Spanish-style house that had been built with two bedrooms and two baths, with a courtyard in front and a nice back yard. Someone had added a master bedroom and bathroom, so we had three bedrooms and three baths.

Although not a large house, it was certainly bigger than our two-bedroom apartment in Queens, which was maybe 1,200 square feet.

We paid $28,000, with $5,000 down. We dealt with the owner, not a real estate agent. We agreed on a price and were about to open escrow when I said to him, "We can only buy it if we can move into the house in two weeks."

He said he wasn't sure the paperwork, title insurance

and inspections would be done that quickly. I said, "I'll buy it right now and give you a deposit, but I have to move in." He reluctantly agreed, and when our furniture arrived, they unloaded it right into the house.

During the week I was out all day, looking for new buildings, and most nights I would be meeting with people over business dinners, trying to get more business. Saturday was my day to be at home, playing with the girls there or taking them to a park. That gave Eris a free day to do whatever she wanted, which often was shopping or running errands. We always spent Sundays together.

On a Saturday a couple of weeks after we moved in, I was in the kitchen with the girls when someone knocked on the front door. I saw a man who looked like a carpenter or workman.

He said, "Are you the one who bought the house?" "Yes." "I'm one of the owners who's selling it to you." I told him I didn't know there was anyone involved other than the young guy we had been dealing with. "That's my partner," he said, and proceeded to tell me what an ungrateful person his partner was.

This guy was an upholsterer who had come from Europe, and had a heavy accent to prove it. He had taught his partner about buying and selling homes, then discovered that his partner had done some other deals without him.

He was really angry. "Let me show you some things he didn't do right." He walked through the house pointing out places where his partner had cut corners on the renovation. There was new plasterboard in the kitchen. He punched his fist through it, and pointed out some mistakes hidden behind it.

Then he looked at the living room and said, "What the hell is the matter with your couch?" There was nothing wrong with the couch. It was just old, and had a big sway in it on the bottom.

I was too embarrassed to admit I couldn't afford to buy a new one. He said, "I'm an upholsterer. I'll come next Saturday and I'll fix it." Then he left.

Eris came back a couple of hours later. The first thing she said was, "Who put the hole in the kitchen wall?" I explained about our visitor, the upholster, and showed her the list of maybe 25 items that I was going to insist the seller fix while the house was still in escrow. Then I said, "He's going to come back and fix our couch."

"Larry," she said, "I can't believe you let this man walk around our house and put a hole in the wall, and you think he's going to come back to fix our couch? Do you even know who he is?"

That was one of the differences between Eris and me: she was much less trusting than I am.

I gave the seller the list of repairs that had to be finished while the house was in escrow. He was very upset, but he had no choice. It took him two months, but he fixed everything. He probably suspected that his partner came by; how else would I have known to punch a hole in the kitchen wall?

The next Saturday, the upholsterer came back and fixed our couch, which enabled us to keep it another five or six years.

I asked him why he pointed out all of these p r o b l e m s . After all, the more money his partner had to spend to fix them, the less the upholsterer made

Californians Lisa, Robyn and me in 1965

from the deal. He understood that, but he was so angry that all he cared about was making sure his partner didn't make money on the sale!

That first house was a very good buy. In fact, all the homes we bought over the years were good buys, and in hindsight I should have kept them all.

But I was not one of those do-it-yourselfers whose clever improvements increase the value of their homes. I owned a screwdriver, a hammer and a couple of wrenches, mostly for use by Eris' uncles, who were all very handy. If they had to come over to fix something, at least I had some tools for them to use.

If Eris asked me to do anything more complicated than changing a light bulb, I would say, "Let's hire somebody. I make too much money to do this myself. It'll take me too long, I'll be aggravated, and I won't do it right."

That didn't always stop her. One day she decided that I should paint the garage. I said I didn't know anything about painting. She said, "Larry, it doesn't take any talent to paint a white garage." One side of the garage faced a neighbor, and the back faced another neighbor, so there was only the front and one side for me to paint.

I said okay, and bought paint, a brush, and a ladder. The next Saturday I painted maybe 20% of the garage – but not from top to bottom. I painted a little over here, and then a little over there, mostly on the front. It didn't look great, even to me. After that I never touched it again.

Eris was pretty upset. "You have to finish the garage, Larry, it looks terrible." I found one excuse after another. I just didn't want to do it. Eris' father, you may remember, was a painter. "If he was alive, he would paint the place," she said. "Then get somebody who worked with your father," I said, and we did.

That was the last time Eris asked me to paint anything.

Buying Property in
Los Angeles

When I arrived in Los Angeles, I started managing buildings for other owners. As with many things in my life, this came about through a friend. When I was in New York, I had done some business with Ben Shore, a mortgage broker, putting him in touch with building owners who wanted to finance or refinance their properties.

Just as I was about to move to Los Angeles, Ben introduced me to a friend of his, Earle Kazis, who managed buildings for owners, including some with very large portfolios.

When Earle heard I was moving West, he said he managed two buildings in Los Angeles. One was owned by the Tisch family through Loews Corp., which at the time owned a chain of over 100 movie theaters. The other was owned by Harry Helmsley, of Helmsley Spear, whose holdings included the Empire State Building.

Earle had someone handling the Los Angeles buildings, but

he was not satisfied with their work.

I'd have to be licensed as a real estate broker in California, but because I had worked in real estate in New York for more than five years and had a law degree, I could take the test as soon as I arrived in California. I took the test, which was almost as tough as the bar exam, and got my broker's license.

Operating as Lawrence N. Field & Associates, I rented an office in the Roosevelt Building, at 727 West Seventh Street. (A beautiful 12-story building in downtown Los Angles, it was designed by the distinguished architectural firm of Curlett and Beelman and built in 1927. It was recently renovated as a loft-style apartment building.)

Over the next couple of years I brought in about 25 additional properties, handling leasing, renovations and other management functions on behalf of their owners.

I immediately saw that real estate prices in Los Angeles were much lower than they were in New York. It was clear to me that Earle and I should go beyond acting as a broker or manager, and own properties ourselves. Earle had his hands full with properties he was buying on the East Coast, so I decided to move ahead on my own, under the name Southland Investment Company.

I bought a number of properties, syndicating them with people I knew. Initially they were mostly from New York, but I soon began working with investors in Los Angeles. Some of my first partners here were people I met at the Los Angeles Athletic Club, which was a short walk from the Roosevelt Building.

I'd go to the club for a workout two or three times a week, at 5:30 in the morning. I'd stay for breakfast, and became friendly with a lot of the people I met there.

Art Miller, who was in the food business, was one of my first investors. He had his accountant check me out, and the accountant recommended me to a client of his, Judith Lubay, a psychiatrist, who became one of my largest investors. Another major investor was Aaron Sobel, an Israeli electrical contractor, with whom we became family friends.

Other early investors were Norman Hinerfeld, who was president of Kayser-Roth Corporation, an apparel company; Bud Mello, an independent sales agent for an electric motor company and a gym buddy; Art Noah, who was in the health food business; Howard Brown, Art's attorney, who only put in $5,000, which in hindsight he of course regrets; my doctor, Ken Matsumoto; my friend Norman Waldman, with whom I bought property in Venice; and my dentist, Alan Zweig.

John Harrington, a friend who was the head of the real estate practice for Price Waterhouse in San Francisco, introduced me to Bob Matousek, who eventually invested in all my deals.

Lillian Sigal, one of Eris' aunts, made a very modest investment; for her sake, I wish she had invested more, but would never press her beyond her comfort level. My cousin Ken Berc became one of my largest investors. Steve Sherman, Ken's brother-in-law, also came in.

Mel Rifkind, my public relations guy, certainly believed our press releases, because he became an investor as well as a good friend.

Lee Meyers, the president of Penn Corporation, which was a tenant in one of our buildings in Santa Monica, invested, and I'm glad he did, because I once flipped a coin with him for a six-month rent increase – and lost.

And of course there have been many others over the years.

I met Isaac Auerbach through our activities on behalf of Ben-Gurion University. Howard and Chris Hirschhorn were close friends from our college days. Jim Schreier was an attorney, and Ron Sunderland was another guy I met at the gym. Jerry Hodes and his then-wife Gayle were my partners in a parking lot project, and Steve Rosenberg and I had partnered on the construction of some houses.

I met Zev Yaroslavsky in 1975 when he was running for the city council. I liked him and supported him, and a couple of years later he become an investor. Zev won his race for the council, did terrific things for the city for nearly 20 years, and was later elected to the powerful County Board of Supervisors, where he served for another two decades, retiring in 2014.

At one of Zev's events, I met a nice guy named Jack Colker.

A few weeks later, Eris came home and told me about a great gas station she had found, where the attendants would wash your windows and check your oil. The owner, she noticed, was wearing a cap that said "Am Yisroel Chai," a Hebrew phrase that means "The Jewish Nation Lives," an expression of pride in and support for Israel.

She said, "You should go there to get gas." I did, and it turned out that the man wearing the cap was Jack Colker, the same nice guy I had met at the Yaroslavsky event. We became close friends, and Jack eventually became one of my largest investors.

Zev was one of the best-known political figures in Los Angeles, but another of my partners is now far more famous.

That is Frank Gehry, the world-renowned architect who designed the Walt Disney Concert Hall, the Guggenheim Museum in Bilbao, Spain, and a great many other amazing and innovative structures.

I'm delighted to say Frank and I have been very close friends for about half our lives. Of course, we were both a lot younger, and much less successful, when we met.

Many of the people who became partners were fascinating individuals from backgrounds very different from mine. Bob Matousek was a bon vivant and wine connoisseur, a charming man of the world who helped build up a very large company that operated duty-free shops in airports and was eventually sold for $4 billion. Bob grew up in Montana, and is something of a cowboy and a wonderful storyteller.

Looking back, it's good to see how my investors have fared. For example Bud Mello, the agent for the electric motor company, invested about $55,000. When he retired, he received roughly $50,000 annually.

The amounts I raised for the properties we acquired in the 1970s were significant at the time, although they seem small today: for the Mississippi Avenue property, $220,000; Stanford Street and Nebraska Avenue, $200,000; 10th Street and Colorado Avenue, $250,000; and 903 Colorado Avenue, $150,000. We purchased these four properties for under $800,000 in cash. Today, of course, they're worth many times that.

Almost every person who invested was someone I knew or got to know. It wasn't like today, when you run some ads or have meetings for people you don't know, and someone gets up and makes a pitch, or you get money from the public through Wall Street firms. When we started out, it was very personal.

In fact, I was so confident in the opportunities I saw that I felt it was a disservice to my closest friends not to ask them, and I felt bad if someone turned me down.

Later, after I had reached a level of success, I didn't take it as personally. If someone wasn't interested, I'd just tell myself – and them – that they were making a mistake.

Of course, after you are really successful and have our kind of track record, nobody turns you down. They understand that I think it's my obligation to take better care of their money than I do of my own.

I don't think that's unusual for people in my position. If somebody entrusts you with investing their money, you are much more careful than if it's your own money.

That's just human nature, and I think there are two reasons for that. First, the vast majority of people are honest, and don't want to take anything that's not theirs. Second, most people don't want the responsibility of taking care of somebody else's possessions.

Eris and the girls in our back yard, 1967

Imagine somebody said to you, "Here is $10,000. I'm going away for a year. You invest it." It's likely you'd tell them to put the money in the bank. Even if you are pretty good at managing your own money, and are comfortable with taking some risk, it's very different when you have to make business decisions that may affect someone else's assets and financial security. It's a burden. But it's one that I and the people who work with me have been willing to take on.

It's been a great pleasure for me, all these years, to make money for other people as well as for myself and my family.

One of my earliest purchases of property in Los Angeles also turned out to be the shortest-lasting and most nerve-wracking. I found two large lots that were available in the mid-Wilshire area. They were near Fremont Place, one of the early gated communities in the city.

The lots, which totaled about 50,000 square feet, could be acquired for $10 a square foot, or a total of $500,000. I thought that was very cheap, especially for a site on which you could build an apartment or office building. You certainly couldn't buy property in Manhattan for $10 a square foot.

I called some real estate people I knew in New York. Zel Kelvin, the head of United Realty Company, was interested. He liked the idea of acquiring properties on the West Coast. I opened escrow on the lots, putting down a $10,000 deposit, and began the due diligence process. United Realty would put in the rest of the money later.

About halfway through the escrow, Zel called me up. He said, "Our board of directors" – all of a sudden he had a board of directors – "feels we should not be building 3,000 miles away." I told him I had already put up the deposit, expecting him to send a check to cover it. What did he want me to do? "I suggest you sell it."

I said okay, if he sent the $10,000 I'd put up for the lots, I'd sell the land and we'd split any profit 50/50. That had been our deal. He never sent the check, and I called him again, saying he wasn't acting like a partner and I was going to sell the land and, if I made any profit, keep all of it. I did sell it, and made about $30,000 on the deal. That was my first real profit in real estate.

I didn't want to sell, because I felt the property was irreplaceable. But I did learn a valuable lesson: buy buildings, not vacant land. If I had been buying a building, I could have easily gotten a loan from a bank for 70% to 80% of the price.

However, when you buy land, you generally have to buy with cash. Banks and insurance companies don't want to lend on land. It's difficult to resell quickly if they have to foreclose, because it generates no income.

The seller normally doesn't want to take back a loan on the land, because in effect he's betting on the buyer's ability to develop the property and make a profit.

Of course, because I had never built a building, there would have been a learning curve while I figured out how to become a developer. I did plenty of that later. But I took away one more lesson from this transaction: if I had to depend on partners to help finance a project, I should get the check first.

Despite the headaches, I felt encouraged in my belief that Los Angeles was a good city to operate in, and that I should be buying more property. So I did.

My next purchase was the Evanston Apartments, also in mid-Wilshire near Vermont, not far from the old Brown Derby Restaurant. A six-story building, it had some retail tenants at the street level. About half of the units were furnished apartments.

I brought in investors as limited partners, people I had met in Los Angeles. The next building we bought was a medical office building on Sixth Street, between Western and Vermont. Things were going very well.

Then I bought the Los Altos Apartments, at 4121 Wilshire Boulevard. Built in 1925, it was – and still is – a gorgeous Spanish-Colonial style building that had been home to Hollywood stars like Clara Bow, Bette Davis, Mae West and Douglas Fairbanks. It's also where William Randolph Hearst and Marion Davies had their trysts. It is now on the National Registry of Historical Landmarks.

But it was showing its age and in need of repair when we bought it. About a year later it was seriously damaged in an earthquake, followed a month later by a fire. I needed a second mortgage to help pay for the repairs, and got it through Stan Glickman of Property Mortgage Company. Stan processed the loan very quickly. I paid it off within a year, and subsequently sold the property. Los Altos had been a star-crossed property, and I was happy to have it off my hands even though I didn't make much money on the sale.

Shortly after this, in 1968, I bought our first large acquisition, a 13-story office building at 6505 Wilshire Boulevard, almost at the intersection of San Vicente Boulevard and Wilshire. Earle Kazis introduced me to W.R. Grace and Company, which became an investor.

I reached out to the head of the real estate department at Bear Stearns, which was then a large Wall Street brokerage house, who I knew from my days in New York. He brought in a number of the firm's senior executives as investors. We raised about $1 million from those two groups, got a loan from a life insurance company, and made the purchase.

There were some very interesting tenants in 6505, including two major advertising agencies: J. Walter Thompson and Doyle Dane Bernbach. I got to meet Ned Doyle, who was an icon in the advertising industry.

His partner, Bill Bernbach, was one of the first well known Jewish advertising guys. Until then, Jews mostly held behind-the-scenes positions. They might be creative directors or copywriters. But they were not account executives. The guys who took clients out for drinks were usually WASPs.

A lot of business got done over cocktails back then. If I wanted to get a mortgage on a piece of property, I would have a drink with the guy from the insurance company. I'd tell him I needed a million dollar loan, where the property was, and what I was planning to do with it.

Loans were made on very flimsy information, and half the time lenders didn't bother verifying the income of the building. That's how business was done. It was who you knew in the business that determined whether you got the loan or not.

When I buy property, I try to buy any adjacent property I can. Next door to 6505 Wilshire was an empty lot, and adjacent to that was a small building. I ended up buying both of them, which meant we needed another partner to provide more money. That partner was Bruce Rosette, who had raised partnership money, primarily for multi-housing. Bruce bought into the Evanston Apartments and the Los Altos Apartments as well as 6505 Wilshire, and moved his company into 6505. Now I had three outside investors, and I owned 25%.

A little while after we had bought 6505 and the two adjacent parcels, two buildings east of 6505 became available. I was not in a position to buy them, but I suggested to the senior executives of Doyle Dane Bernbach, with whom I had become friendly, that they should buy both properties, which were owned by an insurance company.

I was so excited by the opportunity that I declared, "If you don't like them, let me know and I'll buy them myself." They did buy both properties.

Then, a few months later, they called me. "We changed our minds. Buy them from us." That wasn't even the worst of it. Their original plan was to renovate the buildings, so they had told the tenants they had to leave. I told the DDB executives that I would be willing to buy the buildings if they had tenants generating an income for the properties, but I couldn't buy them without tenants, because no bank would lend me the money on empty buildings.

Their lawyer called me and said, "You really are obligated. We can sue you." I said, "I don't think you should," which is not exactly a powerful legal argument. But in the end they didn't sue.

During the process, I became friendly with some attorneys from that firm that was threatening to sue me. One of them was

Me and my gals, in 1968

Gary Handler, a wonderful guy who had a lot of Hollywood stars as clients, including Robert Redford, Barbra Streisand, Sally Field and Sean Connery. Gary later became the head of TriStar Pictures. Tragically, he died of cancer when he was just 50.

In hindsight, I should have taken the risk and bought the buildings even though they were empty. Anything that I could have bought, I should have bought. Whatever I would have paid for properties at that time was nothing in comparison to what they were worth later. I was right about Los Angeles; it was a great city in which to buy buildings. And it still is.

In the early 1970s the economy was in a slump. By 1974 we had owned 6505 Wilshire for several years. Some of the larger tenant leases were coming up for renewal, and my investors were getting restless and wanted us to sell it.

I had paid about $30 a square foot for the building, or about $3 million. It needed some refurbishing, and I would have liked to build on some extra land we owned next to 6505, but we didn't have money for either, and in that market I couldn't raise it. A couple of large tenants, including the advertising agency J. Walter Thompson, had told us they'd be moving out. A branch of Bank of America, which occupied 12,000 square feet on the ground floor, had left for a nearby location, and another small street-level retailer had moved out.

I was at a meeting of The Jewish Federation of Greater Los Angeles, which supports a lot of charitable activity serving both the Jewish and non-Jewish communities, and learned that the Federation needed more office space and was planning to buy a building at 6399 Wilshire, a block away from our building.

I had never thought of the Federation as a possible buyer for 6505, but I realized it would be ideal for their needs. The ground floor space would make a great auditorium for the Federation, there was plenty of office space for its staff, and much more parking than at the 6399 building.

I approached the head of the Federation and said, "I can give you a better deal." When the Federation board heard the proposal, they immediately agreed it was a better building. But half of them were real estate people, and they really hammered me on the price.

I ended up selling it for about the same price we had paid. And on top of that, they extracted some donations from me and my partners, including the officers of W.R. Grace, who were mostly Irish Catholics. As a result, that year W. R. Grace gave a $50,000 donation to the Jewish Federation of Greater Los Angeles.

The Federation also said it would need most of the office space, which meant the existing tenants would have to move out by July 1. J. Walter Thompson, the ad agency, had told me it planned to move to a new building in Century City, but still had a few months on its lease, and was in no rush to leave.

I met with the man who ran the agency, and told him the Jewish Federation would be moving in. He was a very nice man, but he seemed to assume that the arrival of the Federation would mean the lobby would resemble the Lower East Side of New York in the 1930s, with lots of bearded men wearing black hats and women with babushkas on their heads and carrying shopping bags, all talking loudly in Yiddish.

Moving out by July 1 would be fine, he decided.

I suppose I could have pointed out to him that the people visiting the Federation would look just like the people in the lobby of his new building in Century City, or the movie studio executives who were the ad agency's clients. Instead, I simply wished him the best of luck in his new office, and told the Federation that the space they needed would be available.

We didn't make any money on the sale, but it was a terrific deal for the Federation. The building it bought for $3 million, or $30 a square foot, would probably today sell for $900 a square foot or more, or about $90 million. For decades, at least five members of the Federation's board each took credit for coming up with the idea to buy 6505 and getting me to sell the building.

Whenever they did, I agreed with whichever of them was making the claim. There was no reason for me to argue about it. But it certainly proves the truth of the saying that success has many fathers, while failure is an orphan. If something is a success, everyone wants to share in it.

I had very good luck with land in Los Angeles. It was a different story when it came to water.

One of the people I met here was Marshall Fisher, who did

interior office renovation and construction work on some of our buildings. He had an unbelievable design sense, a wonderful eye. I gave him some old wood paneling that had been pulled out of a 1928 building once occupied by the Bank of Italy. He built two beautiful bars from the wood, one for himself and one for me.

A couple of years after we arrived in Los Angeles, Marshall invited Eris and me to join him and his wife, Fran, on a trip to Catalina on their sailboat. When we arrived in Cat Harbor, our plan was to anchor and stay on the boat overnight.

When we went ashore for dinner, Fran called home to check with the babysitter who was watching their three-year-old daughter, Laurie. The babysitter said Laurie had a fever. Fran wanted to go home immediately. The next plane would leave at 2 a.m. Marshall said, "It's only ten o'clock. Why don't we go back under power? We can get back by 3 a.m."

We all got back on the boat. Marshall raised the sail and we left the harbor, but when he tried to start the engine, it wouldn't fire. He worked on it for about half an hour and finally got it started, but it would only work in reverse; we couldn't go forward. We sailed backwards for an hour or so, and then the motor conked out completely. We had the sail up, but there was hardly any wind.

By this time we were miles from the harbor, and couldn't even get back to take the plane. And we were drifting toward Newport Beach, not Los Angeles. Fran was getting frantic. We saw the plane leave right on time, at 2 a.m.

Marshall said, "We'll flag down a boat." We waved at a few passing powerboats, and finally one stopped. We told them Fran had an emergency at home, and they agreed to take her to their destination, which was Newport. Eris went with her. Marshall said to me, "Here, you take the wheel." He was going to use the dinghy to row the women to the other boat.

Coming from the Bronx, I didn't know very much about sailing, including the fact that our boat would keep drifting with the current, away from the powerboat, which revved up and left. The dinghy now was 60 feet away. Even with Marshall shouting instructions, it took about an hour for me to turn our boat around and get close enough for him to row back.

We both had a drink, and he decided to cook some food on a hibachi. By now it was 5 a.m., and there was still no wind. "Look, there's nothing we can do," Marshall said. There was no wind, and no motor. We decided to make an adventure of it, and relaxed. All of a sudden a gust of wind hit the sail, swinging the boom and knocking the hibachi into the ocean.

We drifted all the next day, and around dusk Marshall said, "Ach, Fran has my glasses." He had bad eyes and needed special glasses at night. "I better set our course now, while I can see." That wasn't very reassuring to me, who knew nothing about sailing and was now being asked to steer the boat. We were moving, but very slowly. That night there was a moon, so we could see.

Fran and Eris had arrived in Newport at about 6 a.m., rented a car and drove home. Fran had realized about half an hour after the powerboat picked them up that she had Marshall's night eyeglasses. Going back with the glasses would delay them too much, but they offered to radio Marshall. Naturally, Marshall's radio didn't work. We couldn't call anybody, and they couldn't call us.

Fran phoned the Coast Guard when she got home. They asked Fran if our boat was on fire or there was some other emergency. "No, not when we left." In that case, the Coast Guard said, she should call back if we didn't make it back. They didn't provide towing services to seaworthy sailboats that were inconvenienced by engine problems. By now Eris was also nervous.

Meanwhile, we were working our way back, although at an excruciatingly slow pace. I learned later that there usually isn't much wind after sundown in the patch of ocean between Catalina and the coast. Around four in the morning we were approaching Marina del Rey, where Marshall docked his boat. I had no idea how we were going to get the boat through the narrow channels of the harbor and into his slip without a motor. Marshall wasn't worried. "You're going to do it, Larry, because I can't quite see. I'll just stand in the front and tell you to steer to the left or to the right. Then, when we need to, I'll drop the sails."

He was right, and about five a.m. we docked in Marshall's

slip. I was amazed that I brought the boat in – a boy from the Bronx whose previous seamanship was riding the Staten Island Ferry. We drove home, where Eris was waiting up for me. We never went out on Marshall's boat again, but we did do business together later.

In 1973 I bought my first industrial property, a 15,000 square foot building on Stanford Street at Nebraska Avenue in Santa Monica, with a 30-car parking lot on Berkeley Street. It was one of four buildings owned by a company that made chair glides, gadgets that protect the floor from being gouged by chair legs. After I bought one of the buildings, a second one more than twice as large became available. To raise the money to buy the second building, I syndicated the first one.

I brought in Marshall, despite our disastrous sail to and from Catalina. A second investor was Miles Weiss, who was in the business of repossessing cars, and who later moved his office to the second floor of the building. The third investor was Don Barr, an attorney. Don had a large collection of antique clocks, which he stored in about 7,000 square feet of the building.

Despite that gentle, calm hobby, Don had a take-no-prisoners approach to business, and with his knowledge of the law he let very little stand in the way of achieving his ends.

This property had more security features than any other building I ever owned. Repo men are not particularly popular with the people whose cars they repossess, so Miles set up a security system for his office that resembled something you'd see in an Israeli consulate in a hostile country. He had closed-circuit cameras at the entrances, on the stairs and all around his office. Visitors had to be buzzed in, and when they entered they were in a sealed anteroom. Only after further scrutiny were they allowed in to Miles' actual office.

Chabad

Around this time, there was another parcel of land that was proving difficult to sell. I was partners with Norman Hinerfeld on a property on Fourth Street at Vermont Avenue. We had split the property into three pieces, two with buildings on them, which we sold, and one long, narrow strip of land, about 23,000 square feet, for which we just could not find a buyer.

We had made a nice profit on the other two parcels, maybe $500,000, and I told Norman, "Why don't we just give this away? It doesn't owe us anything." He said, "Fine with me."

I called the Jewish Federation, Jewish Family Services and other nonprofits, but nobody wanted it, because it had an $80,000 loan on it. Then I thought of Rabbi Shlomo Cunin, who was in charge of Chabad activities on the West Coast. Chabad is an Orthodox Jewish movement that quietly does a lot of good in the community.

Rabbi Cunin himself is hardly a quiet guy, however – full of energy, brimming over with ideas, and with a good head for business. Like me, he was a fan of President Reagan. I'd met him a few months earlier. I called him about the piece of land, and he said, "Larry, that's great. I'll be right over."

He arrived with a quitclaim deed, ready to be filled out. That's all he required. He asked what the monthly payments were on the loan, which were about $600, and the property taxes, which were about $6,000 a year. "So the cost is roughly $1,100 a month," he said. "You give us $1,100 a month, we'll own it and use your donations to make the payments."

By giving the land to Chabad, Norman and I took a deduction for the $300,000 fair market value of the land, minus the mortgage, for a net deduction of $220,000, or $110,000 for each of us. At a 40% tax rate, we each saved about $44,000 in taxes. Rabbi Cunin eventually sold the land for about $250,000, so after paying off the mortgage, Chabad got about $170,000 from the transaction.

Rabbi Cunin called with the news about the sale, and said he wanted to present Norman and me with plaques to thank us. Norman, who doesn't make a big deal about being Jewish, said he didn't want a plaque, and I didn't either, but there is no stopping Cunin.

Norman finally told them to mail the plaque to his office in New York. Rabbi Cunin and his people came to my office and made a formal presentation. It was a little loud, and a lot of fun. I put the plaque away in my office, and forgot about it.

Then I got a call from Norman.

Rabbi Cunin had sent a group of Chabad folks to Norman's office at Kayser-Roth Corporation in New York, which was a big apparel company, to present the plaque to him.

"Larry, I got three bearded guys with black hats and coats sitting in the Kayser-Roth waiting room, and everybody keeps coming out to see them. I told my secretary to tell them I wasn't in, but they said they'd wait. An hour later I sent her down again to say she didn't think I was coming in. They said they'd wait 'til we closed, and come back tomorrow. These guys won't leave!"

He finally gave up, and invited them into his office. They gave him the plaque, said a prayer, and offered to lay tefillin (small leather boxes containing parchment scrolls with verses from the Torah and worn by observant Jews during weekday prayers) on him. He says he declined, but knowing how determined Chabad people are, I'm not sure.

I thought *that* was the end of it, but I was wrong again. When Chabad had their annual dinner in Los Angeles, Rabbi Cunin called and said, "I'd like you to come, Larry." I said, "I don't go to dinners." "No, no, no, you've got to come. You're going to honored, the main honoree. This year you gave the most to Chabad as an individual. And you're going to have a table. Bring four more couples."

Eris reluctantly agreed to go, and we invited four couples. When we got to the hotel, I noticed that I was seated at Table 8 along with the other four guys in our group, while Eris and the four women were at Table 17. Just like in Orthodox synagogues, the women and men were seated separately.

Eris had not been happy about going to the dinner in the first place, and understandably this really annoyed her, but she put up with it.

Maybe she was lucky to be sitting at another table, because Cunin came to me and said, "We'd like to carry you in on a chair." That's a traditional way of honoring a person at Jewish celebrations like weddings and bar or bat mitzvahs. But it wasn't for me. I wasn't getting married, and it wasn't my bar mitzvah. No chair for me!

It's not that I was opposed to my donation being acknowledged. I have an ego, like anyone else. In fact, I'm a big believer in putting a major donor's name on the building or wherever. It makes them feel good, it encourages others to give, and in the end, it's just a plaque or a sign. I enjoy supporting good causes. Some people I know buy yachts or expensive cars. They get a kick out of them. I don't.

I really enjoy philanthropy, and so did Eris. Her name and mine are on a number of buildings. There's the Eris Field Plaza at the Walt Disney Concert Hall in Los Angeles, and the Eris M. Field Chair in Diabetic Research at Cedars-Sinai Medical Center, which she established after they helped her manage her diabetes.

Among our other projects are the Lawrence N. Field Center for Entrepreneurship and the Lawrence and Eris Field Building at Baruch College, the Field Medical Simulation Center at Ben-

Gurion University of the Negev in Israel, The Lawrence N. Field West Gate at the Hollywood Bowl, and many others.

If I owned a yacht, I could take a few people out for a sail. At the Field Center for Entrepreneurship, every year hundreds of students and entrepreneurs – many of them immigrants to America, like my father was – learn how to start and run their own businesses.

Over the past 25 years, the Center has helped about 20,000 entrepreneurs, who in turn have created about 7,000 jobs and generated more than $150 million in new business activity. To me, that beats having the best yacht in the world.

"Calling Dr. Field!"

Philanthropy has allowed me to support wonderful men and women who create beautiful music and works of art, teach important skills, cure illness and alleviate pain, and much more. They make a real difference, and indirectly I'm helping them do that.

Once, however, I got to change a life directly, curing a terrible case of jaundice with just a few words. Sort of.

Soon after Eris and I arrived in California, Eris was suffering from severe headaches. We saw one doctor after another, but she didn't improve. My lawyer, Buddy Fischer, suggested we see Dr. Morrie Siegel, because "He's one of the few doctors who takes the time to talk to you." Morrie was a heavyset guy who smoked cigars while he talked to his patients.

He talked with Eris for a very long time, asking her a lot of questions. One was, "Are you taking any medicine? Any pills?" Yes, she was taking birth control pills. Morrie consulted a big pharmacology reference book, and saw that headaches were a rare but known side effect of the birth control pills Eris was taking.

He suggested that she stop taking them for a month, then come back to see him. She did, and within a week the headaches were gone, and they didn't return.

Not surprisingly, Eris decided that Morrie Siegel was the doctor for her, and so did I.

We soon learned that this gentle, caring man was the brother of Bugsy Siegel, the infamous and fearsome gangster who founded Murder Inc., was a hitman for the mob and, on their behalf, built some of the first big casinos in Las Vegas, including the Flamingo. Bugsy, whose real name was Benjamin, was shot to death at the Beverly Hills home of his girlfriend in 1947, two decades before Morrie cured Eris' headaches.

Morrie would never discuss his brother. Bugsy was at least ten years older than Morrie, and provided the money for him to go to medical school.

I saw Morrie a couple of times a year, for checkups. One time, after he had examined me and I was getting ready to leave, he came back into the examining room where I was sitting and said, "Larry, I have a woman here. There's something wrong with her, her thought processes." "What do you mean? She's crazy?" "Well, she's eccentric."

She certainly was. The woman had decided to eat only carrots. For the previous three weeks she'd had eaten nothing but carrots – five to eight carrots for breakfast, lunch and dinner. Not surprisingly, her skin had turned a yellowish orange.

Morrie told her it was because of the carrots, but she was convinced she had jaundice. She had told him, "No, it's not the carrots. My fortuneteller told me carrots are good, eat carrots and you'll never become senile. So it can't be the carrots." Morrie tried a few more times to talk sense to her, but she was convinced it was jaundice, not carrots.

Morrie, thinking quickly, said to her, "You're in luck!" "Why?" "I have a man visiting me right now, Dr. Lawrence Field, who is an expert in tropical diseases, specializing in jaundice. He happens to be in my office. Do you mind if I bring him in to examine you?" She said no, she didn't mind.

He told me all this when he came into the examination room where I was getting ready to leave. He said he'd introduce me as Dr. Field, a specialist in malaria and jaundice. I said, "I don't know anything about jaundice." "Don't worry. She knows less."

We went into the room where she was waiting. Her face, neck and back were a bright orange-yellow. He introduced me, told her how famous I was, then said, "Dr. Field, you've seen this lady and the results of my examination. Do you think that she has jaundice or something else?"

In a very serious voice I asked her, "Have you been eating carrots?" Up to this point, Morrie hadn't said anything in front of her about carrots. She said, "Oh, yes."

I said, "Well, carrots are very good, but if you eat a lot of carrots — I mean a *lot* of carrots — you're going to turn yellow. We found in our experiments that people who had jaundice turned yellow. Then we gave carrots to other people, just to see what would happen, and they also turned yellow. The blood tests Dr. Siegel did on you tell us you don't have jaundice. So, if you don't have jaundice and you're eating a lot of carrots, you're yellow because of the carrots."

She thought about it for a while, then said, "You know, maybe you're right, Dr. Field." I said, "I know I'm right. I've been doing this for 20 years. There isn't anybody who knows more about yellow skin or jaundice than I do."

Then Morrie asked if I thought it would be a good idea for her to stop eating carrots for two or three weeks and see what happened. "Dr. Field" thought this was a good idea. Morrie turned to her and asked, "What do you think, now you have the opinion of the leading expert?" The woman said, "All right, I'll try."

That was Morrie Siegel. He could have simply thrown up his hands at this stubborn, silly woman and said, "Fine, eat carrots and be orange." Instead he came up with an ingenious way to get her to accept that maybe her fortuneteller was wrong, and that a normal diet was a reasonable choice.

Morrie had a long list of well-known people as his patients. I could see why.

Morrie was less successful changing the behavior of Eris' sister, Bobbie. She was a diabetic, requiring insulin, and a heavy smoker. At one point she was so ill that she was hospitalized for four weeks at Cedars-Sinai with cardiac problems. Her heart doctor, Jack Matloff, was Morrie Siegel's close friend.

Morrie, Jack, Eris and I met. I asked if he could do a bypass. No, Jack said, the only thing that could possibly help was a heart transplant, which back then was a brand new technique. But Bobbie was too weak to survive the surgery.

Morrie visited Bobbie every day in the hospital, and Eris was there for three to five hours a day. I think Eris gave her the will to live, because Bobbie did walk out of the hospital. Morrie thought that was a miracle. She lived for another year or so, but wouldn't or couldn't stop smoking.

Eris' only sister died at the age of 42. It was terribly sad, but I saw how important it can be to have someone to support and encourage you. Without Eris' encouragement, helping her to keep going and try harder, I don't think Bobbie would have ever come out of the hospital.

Dick Weiss and the Founding of Richlar

I built up a successful real estate business in the 10 years after we moved to Los Angeles, first managing buildings for others, then buying and syndicating commercial buildings to partners. But the most lucrative thing I ever did was to found the Richlar Partnership in 1976 with Dick Weiss, and build houses. The name was from the first parts of our first names, Richard and Larry.

Dick was brilliant at putting up houses, but he had little in the way of people skills, and was terrified of risk. That's not a great combination for someone in the real estate business, where you have to deal with sellers, buyers, investors, tenants and a lot of other people, and the swings in demand mean you have to be comfortable with risk.

Previously, Dick had been president of Larwin Company, a highly successful homebuilding company. On paper, Dick looked great. Before Larwin, he had been a senior executive at two other big housing companies. Dick had been a Second

Lieutenant in the Marines during World War II, serving on Guam. He got his law degree from the University of Michigan, with honors.

Larwin had been founded in 1948 by Larry Weinberg, who was Dick's brother-in-law. Larry had been so seriously wounded in World War II that the Army classified him as 100% disabled. Despite that, he grew Larwin into the largest privately owned housing company in the nation, building thousands of homes.

In 1969 it was sold to CNA Financial Corporation for $200 million. Larry got about $100 million, and Larry's brother, who also worked at the company, got about the same. But Dick, who had left the company a year before the sale, didn't get anything, although he believed – with some justification – that he had been a big reason Larwin had been so successful.

It turned out that CNA wasn't so great at running insurance companies, which was its main business, and was even worse at running a homebuilding company. The inflation rate rose in the early 1970s, then the Arab Oil Embargo rattled consumer confidence, and the stock market tanked – all of which clobbered the housing market.

CNA, which was in financial trouble because of missteps in its insurance operations, was purchased for pennies on the dollar by Loews Corporation and the Tisch family, for whom I managed office buildings in Los Angeles.

The Tisches knew real estate, and decided to dump Larwin. They offered Dick the company, essentially for free. He'd come back as president of Larwin, and just take over the $120 million debt on Larwin's books, repaying CNA when he sold homes or lots. He didn't have to put up a personal guarantee, so he could just hand Larwin back to CNA if things didn't work out. It was a sweet deal.

Dick didn't do it. He couldn't. He was terrified at the thought of signing a note for $120 million, even when he had no real obligation to repay it. He talked himself out of it. Another executive, a couple of levels below Dick, took over as president of Larwin, and I think after a few years he was worth a quarter of a billion dollars.

After he left Larwin, he joined a small law firm in Beverly

Hills. I met him while I was negotiating to buy some vacant lots in an area just north of Beverly Hills that is now called Deep Canyon. Another guy, Jerry Oren, was also interested in them. Jerry and I decided to work together, and buy all the lots, about 160 in total. Dick was Jerry's lawyer. At a meeting to discuss the deal, Dick said he'd also like to be a partner.

The company that owned the lots had another project that was in financial trouble, and its banks were nervous. One of them, which held a $10 million note on the lots, came to me and said it would lend me $10 million to buy them. It was a nice offer, for two reasons.

One was that it of course would allow us to buy the lots. The second reason was that the same guy, from the same bank, had come to me two years earlier, threatening to foreclose on my home. I had put it up as collateral for a real estate project which, like many others in 1973, was not doing that great.

I had fixed the problem, and he didn't foreclose on my house, but

Dick Weiss and I celebrate at Richlar

it was funny to see him sitting across the desk, asking me to please borrow $10 million.

Meanwhile, Jerry Oren and I were looking to buy all the lots. Jerry said, "Let's bring in Jona Goldrich and Barry Dean," two successful real estate investors. (Jona was a very interesting guy. He was born in Poland in 1927, escaped the Nazis with his brother in 1942, but lost the rest of his family to the Holocaust. He went to Israel, fought in its war for independence, then came to California and went into real estate.)

While we were negotiating on these lots, Dick and I talked about forming a partnership to buy land and build houses. He was still practicing law, but we went out almost every day, looking at lots. We drove around Orange County, San Bernardino, Simi Valley.

Every time he saw a lot he'd say we should buy it. But he just couldn't make a decision.

At the end of October of 1975, while we were driving out to see more lots, I said to him, "We've got to buy something now. If you're not going to do it, then say so."

I thought he was afraid of giving up his job as a lawyer. I told him he could stay with the law firm, and we would just be partners on building homes. But he said he wanted to be a partner in everything, the commercial property as well as the houses. I said, "Okay. That's fine with me."

Silence. Then he said to me, "Why would you want to be my partner?"

I thought it was an odd question, but said, "Because you know how to build houses, and you're smart, you're an attorney." I was moved that a man could be so capable and still have such self-doubt.

We agreed then and there to become partners in business, and one-fourth partners on the hillside lots with Jerry, Jona and Barry. I had already bought seven of the lots. Dick and I decided that I would sell these to raise some additional cash to put into our venture.

Dick suggested we name our partnership Richlar, a using the first syllables of our first names, because he liked the name Larwin, which was derived from Larry Weinberg's first and last names. (I didn't know at the time that Dick hated his brother-in-law.)

He also suggested we each bring in an attorney to negotiate the partnership agreement. I used Ralph Shapiro, a real estate attorney and an outstanding businessman.

Dick's attorney prepared the first draft of the agreement. Ralph and I made some very minor changes and sent it back. Dick wasn't satisfied, and had his lawyer do a second draft, which was fine with us. Then he sent us a third draft, and a fourth and fifth.

Ralph said there was no reason to bother reading the new drafts. It became a dialogue between Dick Weiss and his own attorney. We didn't even bother to give input.

Finally, Dick's own attorney told him, "This is silly. You're changing your own words in each draft." Dick finally signed, and Richlar was in business.

Richlar and our three partners purchased the hillside lots and went into escrow. As we had agreed, Dick and I sold our seven lots to an independent builder to raise some cash.

Our deal with the seller was that of the 150 or so remaining lots, we would take down about 50 lots a year. (A takedown is where you agree to buy a number of lots, but you take ownership of only a part of the total each year, at an agreed-upon price for each portion.)

Our takedown for the first 50 was at $40,000 per lot, for a total of $2 million. The next 50, the following year, would be at $45,000, and the final group in the third year was at $50,000 per lot. Instead of paying the seller interest, the buyer pays higher prices per lot in the later years.

We had four partners, Richlar and the three other guys. The lots would be divided up, which meant 12 or 13 lots per partner for each takedown. Some lots were bigger than others, and some were in better locations. "How are we going to do this?" I asked.

Jona, who even at that time was one of the largest property owners in Southern California, suggested we let Barry Dean divide them up. Jona said that Barry was suspicious of everybody, but that would work to our advantage. We'd have him divide up the parcels into four groups: A, B, C and D. Then we'd put four pieces of paper in a hat, each with a letter on it. We would each draw a piece of paper out of the hat, and that's the group we'd get.

Jona said, "If Barry divides them up, Larry, there won't be ten square feet of difference between the four packages of lots." He was right. Because Barry couldn't control which group he got, he made sure they were all absolutely equal in value.

We had to put up $100,000 for the first takedown, or $25,000 per partner. Dick and I quickly came to the conclusion that we should not build these houses. We decided to sell our position to some local builders, who paid us $750,000 for the position that had cost us $25,000.

Dick's expertise was in building tract homes, 50, 100 or 200 at a time, saving money because of the volume. The hillside lots, overlooking Beverly Hills, called for very nice custom homes. Dick didn't know that market.

The lots would have been very profitable if we had built on them, perhaps by as much as a couple of hundred thousand per lot or even more. But selling them enabled us to get started immediately in building tract homes, about which Dick knew everything.

We used the money from the hillside lots to buy a tract of land in Oxnard, a seaside community in Ventura County about 60 miles northwest of Los Angeles.

Oxnard and Camarillo: of Plots and Plugs

At the time, Oxnard was a lower-income community, and not particularly attractive. Dick once said, "If you wanted to give California an enema, you'd stick it in Oxnard." It was basically a farm community, best known for growing strawberries; they held a Strawberry Festival every year, and still do.

We bought 89 lots on the wrong side of Oxnard. The land was very cheap, which worried Dick, who was nervous about everything.

The general partner of the seller was a woman who met with us in diners and restaurants, looking like a disheveled housewife. Yet one of her partners was a congressman from the Oxnard area. She'd say, "I'll meet you at the Arby's," show up 45 minutes late, and then I'd have to listen to stories about her children.

But the price was so low that I put up with her craziness. We bought the land at less than $3,000 per lot, a total of less than $280,000. We had that in cash, and planned to borrow $1 million to build the houses.

I went to Manufacturers Bank, with whom I'd dealt on other projects, and we gave them our financial statements. The banker said he'd lend us the money. Then he turned to Dick and said, "I noticed that you have ten accounts at ten different savings and loans, each for $100,000." At the time, the government insured each savings account up to $100,000.

Our banker would look good to his bosses if he persuaded Dick to move his million to his bank. "It would be much easier for us to get the loan approved if you would put some money into Manufacturers. We'll give you the same interest."

Dick turned to the man who had offered to lend us $1 million and said, "I don't know about that. If we don't pay you back, you could take my money."

My jaw dropped. I immediately said, "Don, don't worry, Dick is only kidding. He's got a funny sense of humor."

When we were outside I said, "Dick, our partnership is going to be very brief unless you put a minimum of $400,000 into this bank tomorrow. If you don't, our partnership is over." Reluctantly, he did it.

The first houses we built in Oxnard were priced at $28,000. They were on small lots, 5,000 or 6,000 square feet. Building these homes was what Dick was good at – great at, in fact. He could look at an architect's plans and have a picture in his mind of what the house would look like, what it would be like to walk from one room to another.

Dick liked building modestly priced houses. He also felt it was a good business; there were more people who had less money than people who had more money, so the houses would sell even if they weren't in a great location. On that point he was right.

If he had more courage, Dick could have built an amazing business on his own, but I soon realized he was not entrepreneurial. This guy knew the real estate business inside and out, but he never owned any property other than his house, and when his kids grew up he sold the house and never bought another one.

He just was afraid, and never used his own money. That was terrifying to him. He was a businessman who was so nervous about risk that he squirreled away his money in ten savings and loans.

While we were building in Oxnard, a broker showed us some lots in Camarillo, a much more upscale community a few miles closer to Los Angeles. Jack, the man who owned the lots in Camarillo, was a very successful land dealer. He also owned

Breaking ground for Richlar Plaza

Richlar photo

another big tract, with room for 200 or 300 homes, in a better area of Oxnard, and was interested in selling that land to us as well.

Jack lived in Fresno, about 250 miles from Los Angeles, in the San Joaquin Valley, inland from the coast and pretty much in the center of the state. He had an office in Woodland Hills, and flew there from Fresno in his own plane. We spoke to him a few times on the phone, but couldn't arrange a convenient time to meet.

Finally, Dick said, "Larry, I got an appointment with Jack." "That's great," I said. "Go see him and make the deal." "Why don't you come with me?" I said, "Why do both of us have to go? What do I know from land? You're the guy who bought all that land at Larwin."

Except it turned out he never did buy land at Larwin. They had other people who did that, because Dick was not a people person. He built the houses, but he couldn't buy the land; that required dealing with people.

I could see he was nervous, and finally said, "Oh, all right, I'm really busy, but I'll go." The appointment was at four o'clock in Woodland Hills. At a quarter to three, he came into my office. "You ready, Larry?" I said, "No, I've got a three o'clock appointment." "Oh, gee." Then it started to rain. Dick was beside himself.

We didn't leave until after 3:30, which meant we weren't going to make it out to Woodland Hills by four. If Dick hadn't been driving, I think he would have killed me. He kept saying we were going to be half an hour late, maybe 45 minutes, and Jack would have left.

I said, "Dick, how could he be gone? He pilots a small plane. It's pouring down rain. He's not going to leave. I'm sure he has other appointments besides us."

We were half an hour late when we arrived – and the person who had an appointment with Jack before us was still waiting to see him.

When we did finally get to see Jack, I noticed he was wearing a black stocking cap, and peeking out from under it was a bandage.

Before we even sat down, I said, "Where did you get your transplants?" I realized the bandage was covering hair transplants, or plugs as they called them at the time.

He said, "Bosley," which was advertised in the paper. I said, "I just got some in Beverly Hills at a plastic surgeon." He smiled and said, "I figure mine cost less than yours." I said, "I don't think so. Places like Bosley have to pay for those ads. Tell you what. You write down what you paid and I'll write down what I paid."

He said, "I'll bet you a hundred dollars."

Dick looked stunned. He must have been thinking I was crazy. We turned over the papers. My transplants had cost $12 per plug, and Jack had paid $15. He gave me $100, and we continued talking about our hair transplants.

By this time we were pretty relaxed with each other, and I said to him, "Where are you from? How'd you get into this business? How come you live in Fresno?"

It was the same kind of conversation I used to have with buyers when I was selling Dove soap for Lever Brothers. The plugs had broken the ice. We had a bond, were practically brothers.

For the next 45 minutes, we talked about him, his business, how he learned to fly. He asked me about life in the Bronx. By now it was nearly six o'clock. He looked at his watch and said, "I've got somebody waiting that I have to see, and then I'm going to be leaving."

I said, "Okay. Why don't we just wrap it up quickly? I think the last offer we discussed should be acceptable to you."

He said, "It is. I just want it paid in 120 days rather than 150, but I'll give you time for the due diligence."

I said, "Okay, fine. It's a deal."

That was it. Dick Weiss said goodbye, which except for "Hello" was about the only thing he said during the entire meeting. When we were driving back, Dick was quiet for a long time.

He finally said, "That's amazing, Larry. I never could have done that." I said, "What?" "I never would have dreamed... even if I thought it was a hair transplant, I never would have mentioned it." I could, of course, because I had transplants myself.

Buying Jack's property gave us a total of about 400 lots. That gave us the start to the building we did from 1976 to 1980. At the peak of our activity we were building about 250 to 300 houses a year. Over those four years we acquired about 900 lots, and built on about 800 of them.

We were going to build our usual tract houses on the last hundred lots, but the city stopped us. These lots were in the better part of Oxnard, and they wanted more upscale housing. They started changing the requirements for homes on those lots, and while they were making those changes, the housing market cooled off.

By this time it was pretty clear that Dick and I would be going our separate ways. We never did build on those lots. I paid Dick for his half of the value of those lots when we finally split up, and sold them years later.

My breakup with Dick Weiss was a couple of years in the making. The breaking point came in 1979, when we built an office building, Richlar Plaza, and disagreed over how it should be built.

Dick felt more comfortable building with wood rather than steel. He opted to bring in Barry Berkus, a Santa Barbara architect Dick knew from Larwin, who came up with a very unconventional and somewhat impractical design. It was a series of three-story buildings connected with balconies or patios. Even the air conditioning system was odd.

At the time, both the home and commercial markets were softening. We had a hard time finding tenants for Richlar Plaza, and finally decided to sell it.

At the bottom of the market, primarily through my efforts, we sold it to Stewart Resnick, who owned Teleflora, a florist. (He later owned the Franklin Mint, POM Wonderful, Fiji Water and other companies.)

I put in a proviso that, if we found tenants for the building after the sale, we would get a fee. I did the leasing myself, and we ended up with another $1 million.

Dick and I didn't end our partnership over business issues. He was just a very difficult man to be around. For example, at a meeting with the Bank of America, when we were trying to land a big loan, the banker said, "We submitted it to San Francisco and I think we can do it."

Dick looked at him – a man we had only met once before – and said, "I don't think you'll be able to do it. It's too complicated for you. You'll never understand it."

Needless to say, we never heard from the bank.

Another time he tried to fire my secretary, who was terrific, without even telling me.

He went to extremes about so many things, and he had a hard time with people. Yet he was brilliant at what he did.

The dust had settled. We had stopped building homes in Oxnard and Camarillo. Dick had nothing to do. He didn't manage the properties we owned. It was awkward in the office. He had lost interest in the business. He had made more money in four and a half years with Richlar than he had in 30 years working for his brother-in law.

During 1981, almost all we did was clean stuff up. We both knew we weren't going to continue on together. It finally happened. He said, "I want you to buy me out."

We formally dissolved our partnership in 1982. We told our accountants to figure out what his half of the partnership was worth. Dick would keep half of that amount, and his wife Sue would get the other half. (She remained a partner in my business.)

We met in a conference room to finalize the deal.

His parting shot was pure Dick Weiss. "Well, of course, you can't use the name Richlar Partnership anymore."

Dick Weiss and I at the nearly-completed Richlar Plaza
Richlar photo

I said, "What? Are you going to use it? Some of the limited partnerships use Richlar as the general partner, so we have to keep that. And it's the name on some of the buildings."

He said, "That's okay. But you can't do any new deals." "Why?" He said, "I don't want you to bring into disrepute a name that's half mine."

Dick and I did not stay in touch after we ended our partnership, but he did seem to make a fresh start.

He and his new wife, Maryanne, who was quite entrepreneurial, moved to Colorado, where they started a jewelry company and developed some upscale homes. They later moved to Arizona, where Dick passed away in 2016 at the age of 92. He and Maryanne had been married for 34 years.

Those Richlar years, from 1976 to 1980, were an amazing time.

Whatever we priced the houses at, we sold them for more. When we finished a new group of homes, we would sell ten at $62,000. They sold so quickly that we'd price the next ten at $69,000, then $79,000, and $99,000.

In the space of four years we made maybe $30 million. We weren't a big homebuilding company. We were just two guys, a bookkeeper and a couple of secretaries.

Our houses won a number of awards. For all of Dick Weiss' *mishigas*, he was just fabulous at building houses. They might not have been luxurious, but they were sturdy. We built more than 800 houses by the time we were through, and we never had a single lawsuit.

My concept was to use the cash from the houses to buy commercial properties. Everything changes in real estate, but well-located property will stay with you and add to your wealth as long as you live.

I am a history buff, and I learned early on that the wealthiest families— not only in Europe, but also in New York—controlled large blocks of land with commercial buildings on them. If you hold property free and clear and pass it down to your heirs, it will be with them for their lifetimes.

The English feel very strongly about this. Much of the land in London is leased to the companies that have built office towers on it, because the old families won't sell.

We were making all this money with the houses, but I knew what was lacking was something that would generate a continuing flow of cash. When you own commercial buildings or apartments, the rent you collect enables you to maintain the building and pay back the lenders, and over time you build up equity.

Once you have the building up and running, you receive a steady cash flow that covers your overhead and allows you to pay yourself an income. Meanwhile, the buildings are likely to steadily gain in value.

It's a simple but powerful formula that has built countless fortunes.

By The Beach

In 1977, in the heyday of my time with Dick, we began to use the money pouring in from the sale of hundreds of homes to buy office buildings, warehouses and shopping centers for Richlar. Our largest purchase was land owned by Southern California Gas Co. in the Venice area of Los Angeles, near the beach.

It was two square blocks, about seven acres, between Rose Avenue on the north and Sunset Avenue on the south, and Main Street and Third Avenue on the east and west.

There were two parcels that were not owned by the gas company. One belonged to a man who planned to build a laundromat. A second had been owned by an elderly woman who inherited it from her husband, and which she had donated to her church in return for an income from it during her lifetime.

We agreed to pay $1 million to the gas company, $40,000 to the laundromat guy, and $200,000 to the church, which would in turn take care of the woman. We didn't have a million-plus in cash, and couldn't borrow it, because our money was tied up buying land to build houses. You can borrow the construction money you need to build, but generally you need to have cash to purchase the land.

I signed the contracts with the gas company, the laundromat guy and the church, and we put $50,000 into escrow. We had six months to close, at which point we'd have to come up with the rest of the money.

All during that time I tried to find a buyer for part of the seven acres, to cover at least some of what we would have to pay. I figured we could borrow the rest.

That's when I met Frank Gehry.

At the time, Frank had a small architectural practice. He had been hired by Fred Weisman, the president of Hunt Foods and the brother-in-law of Norton Simon, the billionaire industrialist. Fred was a very wealthy man and a patron of the arts. He wanted to build a museum to house his art, and had hired Frank to design it.

We negotiated to sell Fred one acre on Main Street, a very desirable location, for $500,000.

When it was time to close escrow, the gas company realized they hadn't yet found a place to park their work trucks. We made a deal.

We gave them Fred Weisman's $500,000, and took possession of the property. We would owe them the rest, at no interest. They could park their trucks on half of the property, and pay the property taxes while they were using it. They parked their trucks there for about nine months. In the meantime, we had full use of the rest of the property.

We then negotiated to build a building for Nabisco in a back portion of the land, for the production of their Rose Milk brand hand cream and lotion.

Our plan was to build a two-story building on Main Street, designed by Frank, to house Fred's museum and some shops.

But the residents of Venice were fiercely opposed to the project, claiming we were going to put up a high-rise that would ruin the neighborhood. We could not get approval from the city, and eventually Fred had to abandon the project.

It would have been a beautiful museum, and a real addition to Venice, but it wasn't meant to be.

But there is an upside, because if we had gone ahead with the project, we would have had to tear down the building which is now the Rose Cafe. It was originally some kind of substation for the gas company, about 4,000 square feet. It's been renovated on the inside, but the building itself is like a fortress, unbelievably solid. The Rose Cafe will stand another 50 years.

Fred Weisman didn't get to build his museum, but a little while later I got to reconnect with his architect, Frank Gehry, who needed more space for his practice. He and a friend of his, the artist Chuck Arnoldi, had found a building on Brooks Avenue that they thought would work.

Frank and I knew each other pretty well from our meetings about Weisman's museum project, and they came to me with a proposition. Their idea was that Frank and Chuck, or the two of them and I, would buy the building, with me putting up the money and them paying me back through the rent payments.

I smiled at Frank, who seemed to be leading the discussion, and said, "You guys don't know much about real estate finance, do you?" He admitted they didn't.

I told them they should just get a mortgage from a bank, buy the building themselves, and pay the mortgage with the money they would otherwise pay a landlord as rent.

I liked Frank, which is pretty typical for everyone who meets him, and it was clear he was a hard worker.

I picked up the phone and called my loan officer at Union Bank, where I was a pretty good customer. "I'm sending you an architect and an artist who need a loan to buy a building. It would be a real favor if you helped them out."

Frank and Chuck got the building, and Frank later told me I was the first real estate developer he'd met who hadn't tried to screw him over.

Later, after both his practice and renown had grown, Frank began investing in my partnerships.

In 2002, we partnered to buy the BMW warehouse on Beatrice Street in Playa Vista, which he redesigned to serve as a studio for what was by then his 150-person team. He took one half of the building. The ad agency Chiat\Day rented the other 43,000 square feet.

In 2008, he and I bought 12 acres in El Segundo, occupied by several large industrial buildings and warehouses, and we created a campus of creative office buildings.

Turning back to Richlar's activities in Venice, I built the Nabisco plant, then the building that housed Gold's Gym. The gym was owned by Peter Grymkowski, a Mr. World bodybuilding champion, and a couple of partners.

They leased about 8,000 square feet, and over several years, as the gym got busier and busier, they gradually took over the entire 40,000 square feet, where the gym still is today.

The Rose Café, a Venice landmark

They opened up a lot of franchises across the country and around the world, then started selling athletic clothing with their logo. They made a fortune. They sold the company in 1999 for more than $50 million.

Gold's Gym was the first time I tried to buy into a company. When we were negotiating their lease, I offered to charge them a lower rent in return for 5% of the company. In addition to being a great bodybuilder, Pete Grymkowski was also a good businessman, because he was smart enough to not give away a piece of his company.

At about the same time, we were working on what is now the Rose Cafe.

Two young men from India, Lareesh Omargon and Manhar Patel, who had studied computer science at UCLA, leased the building to open the cafe. The rent was pretty modest, probably a couple of thousand dollars a month.

They called it the Rose Cafe because it was on Rose Avenue. Lareesh later decided to leave, and Kamal Kapur, who was also from India, joined Manhar and played a key role in its success.

We had one falling out with them, when I tried to get the building back. I had the brilliant idea of tearing it down to build something else. We went back and forth with our lawyers, but fortunately sanity prevailed, and I realized we should leave it. Today the Rose Café is an institution, and for decades I would go there all the time.

The last building we worked on was at the corner of Main Street. It had a few tenants, but the one that occupied most of the space was a company that made gold electrical connectors for aircraft.

The owner, Milt, was an odd guy who walked around wearing riding boots and jodhpurs, those close-fitting trousers for horseback riding, carrying a leather riding crop. Even for bohemian-loving Venice, this was pretty far out.

The company's lease was about to expire. Luckily, I was introduced to Jeff Ayeroff, who was a co-founder of Virgin Records, which was owned by Richard Branson. Jeff thought the building would be great for Virgin. We negotiated a sale price that would give us an outrageous profit.

Everything was set, until Milt refused to leave. His new location, which had double the space, wasn't ready yet. It took us eight months of negotiations and legal threats to finally get him out.

Then we learned that Virgin's parent company was considering a possible sale of the record label to another company. That meant Virgin's executives had to put the brakes on any big purchase, so we didn't make the sale.

We filed a lawsuit, and ended up with a $1 million settlement. It wasn't the fat profit that had been dangling just out of reach, but that was just as well. I could have bought something else with the money, but it wouldn't have been as good as what's there.

We still have all the original properties we acquired in Venice, and we added two more parcels on Third Street for parking.

Around the end of 1986, the Nabisco lease was ending and I was looking around for a new tenant for the 42,000 square feet of space.

I got introduced to the advertising agency Chiat\Day, which was occupying space at the Biltmore Hotel. At that time, the downtown hotels were dying and had loads of space for boardrooms and offices.

Jay Chiat, a brilliant advertising guy, formed the agency with Guy Day in Los Angeles in 1962. The firm had built up a roster of clients including Apple Computer, Nike, Energizer, American Express, Reebok and others. They did the groundbreaking "1984" Super Bowl ad for Apple, and in 1989 were named U.S. Ad Agency of the Decade.

Jay was interested in the Nabisco building and a property we owned next to it. We negotiated a deal to lease them the whole parcel.

Frank Gehry and Jay Chiat were good friends, and Frank designed the building, which won all sorts of awards. In one area that has 30-foot ceilings, Frank designed a conference room that looks like a fish. It is 40 feet by 25, with a table in the center. If people are sitting around the table talking and you are standing at the entrance, the mouth of the fish, you can't hear what they are saying. You hear sounds, but you can't make out the words. It's a brilliant design.

Later, Chiat\Day was acquired by a bigger agency, TBWA Worldwide, which in turn was acquired by Omnicom, a global marketing company. By this time Chiat\Day had moved to a new building, so their place was empty, with three years left on the lease at $500,000 a year.

I went to them and said, "Why don't you give us a million dollars and we'll terminate the lease? You're not using it." The man I was dealing with stalled for months, avoiding my calls and giving me all kinds of stories.

Finally he admitted that Omnicom was so big that a million dollars was too small to get anybody's attention. They continued paying $500,000 a year for an empty building until their lease was up.

Another Venice property that had a somewhat convoluted path to success was the Park Plaza, on the Venice Boardwalk.

Norman Waldman, Shelly Appel and I bought three parcels from Werner Scharff, with plans to build about 100,000 square feet of mixed use space. Before we closed, the city changed the rules so we couldn't build that much.

I went back to Werner and demanded that he lower the price. He said no, and we sued, despite my belief that in a lawsuit both sides usually lose; it's mostly the lawyers who benefit when you go to court.

Werner was a fascinating guy. He was born in Germany, in 1916, and came to New York in 1937, with his brother. They became friends with another refugee, Sepp Lanz, and the three moved to California, where they started the company that sold Lanz nightgowns.

Werner, who never finished high school in Germany, was one of the smartest men I've ever met. He started buying property in Venice in the 1940s, when no one else would touch it. He figured you can't go wrong with beachfront

The famous 'Larry wave'.

property. He eventually owned well over 100 buildings.

Werner didn't get upset when I threatened to sue him. He just told me I would probably lose the lawsuit, so he'd wind up taking the property back. But instead he offered to buy back 50%, so he'd own half and the three of us would own the other half. That made sense, so we all agreed.

There were three parcels. We built a shopping center on one, some condominiums on a second, and we left a piece of land vacant. It turned out to be exceedingly valuable. Werner made a lot of money, and so did we.

We eventually sold the vacant lot, which was about 10,000 square feet, and also sold the 10 condos we built, which we called Thornton Lofts. We kept the shopping center.

Werner was a brilliant businessman, and a real patron of the arts; he hired artists to paint murals on a number of his buildings in Venice. When Werner died in 2006, at 90, the famous muralist Rip Cronk said, "I owe my career to him."

Our Saturday breakfast group at the Nate 'n' Al Deli

He was really a special person, and we were friends until the day he died.

Shelly Appel was the opposite of Werner – he sued over everything. Shelly and I had bought some land to build houses, and had borrowed about $4 million from Chase Manhattan Bank for the construction.

Every year we'd roll over the loan, but then Chase decided to stop lending on real estate in California, and told us we wouldn't be able to renew the loan.

Shelly wanted to sue the bank. For what? They had every right to decide not to renew the loan. But he insisted we see a lawyer we both knew. We had lunch with the attorney, and explained the whole thing. He said he'd need a retainer of $50,000 to take the case.

I told him, "I want you to know that my partner is very litigious, and if you take this case and lose, my partner will probably sue you – and win." The lawyer turned white, and left.

Then I said to Shelly, "let's deal with the bank ourselves," which we did. The bank ended us giving a loan for a couple of hundred thousand less than before, but it was enough for us to continue work. We ended up making about $10 million on that property.

Despite his willingness to sue over almost anything, I really liked Shelly. He was one of the guys who became part of the Realty Group, which I started in 1972. I modeled it after real estate industry lunches that Harry Helmsley would hold in his building at 60 East 42nd Street in New York.

We began meeting monthly at Nibbler's Restaurant on Wilshire in Beverly Hills. In addition to me and Shelly, the original members of the group included Gil Dembo, John Liebes, Bob Crane, Jerry Asher and Bob Cohen. Later we were joined by Dave Altemus, Stanley Black, Jerry Felsenthal, Rick Gleitman, Steve Gordon, Cindy Gray, Arnold Rosenstein, Ken Ruby, Bob Schwab, Ron Simms, Kenneth Weiss and Dick Ziman.

After a few years we decided to move the meetings to the Four Seasons Hotel, where the group – now limited to 15 – continues to meet today.

I've made a lot of good friends in the real estate business. In 1971 or so someone invited me to have breakfast with Stanley Black on a Saturday at Nate 'n' Al's. Mike Schwab, Leo Bromberg and a couple of others were there as well. We've continued to meet there every Saturday, for nearly 50 years.

Stanley is a wonderful guy. He is very friendly, and open to anyone, successful or not, thieves, snobs, everyone. I remember inviting him and his wife, Joyce, to Matteo's soon after it opened on Beverly Blvd.

What I didn't know was that when anyone visited Stanley,

he'd invite them to come along to where he was going, so along with Stanley and Joyce, a dozen other people showed up!

Stanley led a group of guys who would go on fishing trips to Puerto Vallarta every year, and he invited me to join them. We'd leave on a Sunday and come back on Friday, spending six days in Mexico. Dick Waldron, a banker, and Jim Cook, an attorney were some of my friends who came along.

It was a great way to relax, except for the time I got put in the Puerto Vallarta jail.

We had just checked out of our hotel. I had acted as treasurer, collecting money from all the guys to pay for the food and entertainment. I was standing in the lobby with Jerry Wexler when the police showed up, saying we had given a counterfeit $20 to the mariachi players. It was a bill we had received from the hotel as change when we paid the hotel bill.

They arrested us, saying they were charging us with distributing counterfeit bills. Jerry turned white. Mike Schwab saw it happen, and alerted the other guys.

They took me and Jerry to jail in a taxi – and made us pay for the cab.

The whole jail was about the size of my office. The police chief came in, along with a guy from Texas who happened to be there on vacation and spoke both Spanish and English. He told the police we were big shots from California, and knew the president of the United States.

As it turns out, the bill wasn't counterfeit; it was just a very old bill with a design quite different from US currency of the time.

They let us go, and Mike and the rest of the guys picked us up at the jail. We didn't stop until we got to the airport. To this day Mike still talks about our brush with Mexican justice.

I have a lot of great memories from my more than six decades in the real estate business. But even in my late eighties, I'm not ready to retire. I love what I do, and with the help of the great team of people who work with me, I am now busy with two of the most exciting projects of my career.

Some years ago, in El Segundo, a once-dreary industrial community south of Santa Monica, we began repurposing a number of warehouses into creative office space, creating an exciting campus that has contributed to the dramatic resurgence of the city as scores of media and technology companies have made it their home.

As I write this, we have just completed a building that is especially exciting for me because I was able to persuade Frank Gehry to design it. It's the first time in our 40-year-plus friendship that Frank has done a building for NSB. His son, Sam Gehry, oversaw the project.

Called "Ascend", the building has 80,000 square feet of space flooded with daylight via skylights and huge windows opening onto 16,000 square feet of balcony patios.

It doesn't look anything like the Walt Disney Concert Hall in Los Angeles, the Guggenheim Museum Bilbao, or other visually striking landmarks for which Frank is known.

As he explained to the Los Angeles Times, "It's not architectural in the sense that you are making an architectural statement. It is really creating an environment that energizes and promotes interactivity in a less formal way."

I think it's gorgeous.

The Origins of Not So Bad!

When we started the Richlar Partnership, everything seemed to go right. In 1977, from a standing start, our net profit was about $3 million. The next year it was five, then seven million. We were making more money than many public companies. Just two guys, with a staff of eight or nine people. It was unbelievable.

When people asked me how things were going, I would say, "Wonderful," or, "outstanding" or, "couldn't be better." And it really was. Then, for some reason, I started answering with "Not so bad!" People would smile at the joking understatement, and I began saying it more and more.

For reasons I still don't understand, it seemed to be infectious. People who live in other cities and states actually asked me if they could use it, as if I had the trademark. I gave "franchise rights" to friends in New York, Chicago, San Diego and countless other places.

"Not So Bad" became part of me, and I used it everywhere, with friends and strangers. Whenever someone asked how I was doing, how I felt, how the business was going, I'd say "Not so bad" – and I still do. It just feels right.

When Dick Weiss and I split up, and he wouldn't allow me to use the Richlar name in my future business dealings, I said to Eris, "Well, I need a name for my business." I didn't want to use Field or Field Associates, because I wanted something with a broader connotation, in case the company grew to the point where others could be involved in running it.

Eris said, "Well, maybe you should try a little whimsy. You've been using this expression "Not So Bad" for a long time. Why don't you just call the company NSB? Don't say 'Not So Bad,' just use the initials. You know, CBS, NBC, ABC, IBM, all of them just use the initials." I said, "Gee, that's an idea."

Then Eris said, "I bet half the people who know you well, who always hear you say 'Not So Bad,' will have no idea that it's why your company is called NSB. They won't put it together."

She was absolutely right. Except it wasn't half the people; it was more like 95% who didn't figure it out. And once I told them NSB stands for "Not So Bad," it always got a chuckle. For years, my bank didn't know, and some partners didn't know. Even today people come up and say, "You know, all these years I never knew NSB stood for 'Not So Bad'!" People like a little whimsy, and they never forget it once they find out.

Now everybody expects to hear me say "Not So Bad." Every once in a while, if I'm thinking about something else, I might say, "Yeah, I'm okay, I'm fine." The immediate reaction is, "What? Are you okay? You didn't say 'not so bad!'"

So that's how my company became NSB Associates.

Larry Field, Cowboy

One of the nice things about writing your autobiography is that you can talk about how smart you are, and I admit to doing some of that in these pages. But as my parents and Mr. Birnbaum taught me when I was five years old, you have to tell the truth. So let me tell you about Larry Field, The Cowboy.

As you can imagine, growing up in the Bronx I didn't know much about cattle. As an adult in Beverly Hills, I knew even less. But in the early 1980s I was making a lot of money from real estate ventures, and paying a lot of taxes. So when I met a man who was touting a tax shelter, I was interested. To avoid embarrassing his family, some of whom he ensnared in his scheme, I'll refer to him here simply as "Michael."

The idea sounded reasonable. It involved artificial insemination of cows with the sperm of prize bulls. In the laboratory, they would fertilize an egg from a prize cow with the sperm of an equally special bull. Then they would stick the fertilized eggs into an ordinary cow, who would serve as a surrogate mother. Out of that ordinary cow would pop a champion cow or bull.

And, thanks to our nation's complicated tax code and some smart accountants, we investors would get a big tax write-off.

I was sold on the idea, and put up about $320,000. (To put that in perspective, that's about what my father made, in total, during all the years he ran his grocery store.)

Two other investors, Herb Glazer and Irwin Goldenberg, put in about $100,000 each, so we had more than half a million bucks to start breeding the stars of the bovine world.

Even though I knew nothing about cattle, I should have known better. Whenever Michael came for a meeting, he arrived in a chauffeur-driven limousine. In my book, that's a bad sign.

He was from Orange County, less than an hour from my office, so it would have been easy for me to check him out, but foolishly I didn't. I would have discovered that he didn't own anything in his own name— no house, no car, nothing. Everything was in his wife's name.

He had a ranch in Texas to raise the cows and bulls. I actually flew down to the ranch, which was in Mineola, outside of Tyler, and met the people, who were very nice. It was a big ranch, with about 2,000 head, only a few of which were ours.

I found it fascinating. I saw how they used a special spray to get a cow to "adopt" a calf that wasn't being nursed by its own mother, and learned about how they moved the cows to El Paso for slaughter.

I'd visit with the guys in the bunkhouse. I even had a cowboy hat. I loved the whole thing!

On one trip I brought along my accountant. He didn't know any more about cattle or ranches than I did, but he did know a great write-off when he saw one.

Even putting aside my failure to check out the guy peddling the tax shelter, I should have realized that the plan didn't make business sense.

After all, if you can take half a dozen prize bulls and use their sperm to make thousands of prize calves, it won't be long before you, and other people doing the same thing, turn out enough prize calves not just for the United States, but for the whole world.

Things started to go wrong long before that could happen.

When we had 80 prize calves, Michael ran out of money. He

could not pay to keep the ranch operating, which is when we found out that he didn't own the ranch, he just leased it. We got a notice that the banks were going to foreclose on the ranch.

We quickly discovered that, in Texas, when banks foreclose on a ranch, they have the right to take everything as security for their loan. They didn't care that the 80 cows and bulls we had there didn't belong to the ranch.

Herb, one of the other investors, knew an attorney in Texas. We hired him, and he convinced a judge to give us a little time to remove our cattle.

That was great, but where do you put 80 cows and bulls? Then I remembered that a guy who worked for one of my tenants had told me his family had a ranch in that part of Texas. He agreed to keep them for us, for $30 per month for each animal.

When I wasn't losing money on cattle, I had equal non-success with horses

He sent over some trucks to pick them up, but they could only locate 62 calves. Somehow 18 could not be found.

We started sending him $2,000 a month for room and board for the 62 they did round up.

Then he called and said he'd give us a discount if we'd let him breed his cows with some of our bulls. We agreed. These bulls, with the finest bloodlines, scientifically bred with the latest technology and valued at thousands of dollars each, were doing what comes naturally for less than a buck a day.

If the bulls felt any shame it didn't last long, because the rancher called up a couple of months later and said, "We don't need your bulls anymore. All of our cows are pregnant. You can take your cattle back."

I said, "What am I going to do with them?" He said, "Bring them to Beverly Hills."

I could picture Eris' reaction if trucks pulled up to our house and cows and bulls started meandering into our backyard.

We sold the 62 head for about $200 each, or about $12,000 total. That's what was left of our half a million, not counting the cost of trucking and boarding the cattle, paying the attorney in Texas, and so on.

I was determined not to let Michael get away with it. We sued him for fraud, and sued his son as well, because the son was listed as vice president, even though he was only about 21 or 22, and was basically a messenger who brought us papers to sign.

In the busy Los Angeles court system, it took about two years to get a court date. A month before we were scheduled for a pretrial hearing, I bumped into Michael at a party. He didn't apologize. He just said, "Yeah, well, what are you going to do." I said, "What I am going to do is make sure you go to jail."

Our judge, Bob Weil, held a settlement hearing. He listened to what we said had happened, and to the other side's defense. He told us they weren't willing to settle, and anyway they probably had few assets we could go after.

I said, "What about his son? Can you tell him that if he's convicted his son could also be in trouble?" Bob said that was technically true, but a smart attorney could probably get the son off. Still, he went back to Michael and said, "If you're found guilty, your son could face serious problems too. Do you want to risk that?" It turned out that he didn't. We ended up getting a settlement for a little over $300,000, which under the circumstances I thought was fabulous.

We drew up an agreement, approved by the court, for Michael to pay us $2,500 a month, and if he failed to pay we could bring him and his son back to court. It took about ten years, but we collected $2,500 every month.

Breaking the Bank

In the early 1980s, a friend said he was going to start a savings and loan association. An S&L is sort of like a bank. It accepts deposits into savings accounts, but it primarily makes loans on property – mortgages – rather than the business loans and many other products a regular bank can offer.

The government had eased the rules for forming an S&L. You only needed three or four people. Big investors liked owning an S&L, because for every dollar of capital you put in, the government let you lend five or six. If you put $100 million into an S&L, it could lend $600 million – and could even make loans to the people who formed it as well as their friends and associates. If you owned an S&L and wanted to buy property, you could use your S&L as a vehicle.

Investors caught on quickly. Federal regulators were a lot slower. They were used to dealing with bankers, who by nature were very cautious. The people starting S&Ls were not, and some were downright unscrupulous. And a lot of not-so-knowledgeable guys got into the S&L business – like me.

I can't blame anybody, because I was the one who thought of

it. I told my friend Ralph Shapiro, who was the general partner of the building where I have NSB's offices, about my plan.

He said, "Larry, you're not going to run it, are you?" I said, "No. Stan Glickman has talked to me about it." Ralph said, "Yeah, Stan would be a good guy to do it. It's his business. He lends money."

Absolutely true, and as it would turn out, absolutely disastrous.

Stan ran a very successful company, Property Mortgage Company, or PMC, that made second mortgages. Founded by him and his father-in-law, Elliot Fine, it had been in business for 25 years. It had a $200 million loan portfolio, and a wonderful reputation.

All his money came from private investors, people like my wife, her aunts and relatives, ordinary people who normally would put their money in a bank, but were attracted by the higher interest rates Property Mortgage paid them.

Stan was very enthusiastic about forming what we named Sherman Oaks Savings & Loan. In fact, he didn't want to wait to form it, so we bought one that had already gotten a charter, but needed some additional approvals.

I wanted to just be a depositor, not an investor, but Stan and Ralph were eager to start, so I agreed. I invested about $100,000, and brought in one or two other investors. Ralph did the same, while Stan brought in 10 or 15. He knew a lot of affluent people who had money at PMC, and he was a member of a prestigious country club, where he met more.

Stan, I, Stan's father-in-law Elliot, the president of the S&L, and our controller comprised the board of directors.

It wasn't a big S&L. I think we were listed at $50 million in capital, and that included a lot of goodwill, because our investors had put up a total of maybe $15 million.

Because I was in the real estate business, I reviewed any application for a large real estate loan. Once a week, the vice president in charge of lending would bring me a batch of applications, with information about the various properties, and I would look them over.

I wanted us to stick to residential loans, which are the most conservative because people will do almost anything to keep their homes. You make more money with commercial property loans, but residential is less risky.

I discovered that the S&L was making some commercial property loans that I just couldn't understand. I told the vice president that one in particular made no sense to me, because it had no major tenants. I was in the real estate business, and I certainly wouldn't buy it.

Looking into a residential loan that struck me as questionable, I drove out to see a property that was way out in Thousand Palms, a remote area of the desert. It was an old, odd house on 10 acres – not easy to resell if we had to foreclose. I couldn't understand why we were making these loans, but the guys approving them always had a reason.

Eventually a far more serious problem came to light. Stan had been taking money from his company, Property Mortgage.

Stan started out as a straight, very smart guy. But he socialized with friends who were much wealthier than he was, and he wanted to live like them.

PMC had $200 million of other people's money, but he got only about one percent to manage that money, plus some escrow and other fees. Property Mortgage had expenses, and a staff that had to be paid. One percent on $200 million is only $2 million. Even if you add in some fee income, it's not a lot when you have a significant payroll.

Stan made a nice living, but his friends had businesses that were paying them millions each year. To keep up with their lifestyles, Stan began taking money out of PMC that belonged to his investors. Eventually he could no longer pay his investors the interest they were expecting to get.

Early in 1991, Property Mortgage held a big meeting at a hotel which was attended by 300 of its investors, where Stan admitted they would not be able to pay back everything the investors were owed. The company just didn't have the money.

I went to the meeting and was in a state of shock – my God, he's the chairman of our S&L!

I discovered that, unbeknownst to me, our S&L had bought some of PMC's loans – not a lot, about a million and a half dollars. That gave Stan some cash, but he didn't put it back into the company.

My first concern was that, if Stan had done something wrong at our S&L, it could be a federal crime. He'd be facing jail time. I knew federal regulators would take a very close look at Sherman Oaks S&L because of Stan's position with us.

Even after the meeting at the hotel, I wasn't sure what had gone wrong at PMC. I thought maybe they had priced some loans wrong and couldn't pay back some investors.

But officials discovered it was far worse. The company had been losing money since 1986, and had racked up losses of over $23 million by the time things fell apart. More than three quarters of its loans were non-performing, meaning borrowers were either behind in their payments or not paying at all.

But for five years the company had continued sending out interest payments as if nothing was wrong, using money from new investors.

Property Mortgage went bankrupt. Hundreds of investors, mostly elderly people who had trusted the company with their hard-earned savings, got back only about a third of what was owed to them. In 1998, Stan was sentenced to four years in prison. His father-in-law, Elliot Fine, died four years after the fraud unraveled; the Fine family lost about $10 million.

Stan was done in by envy. He wanted to have a big boat, a nicer house, and live like his very wealthy friends. But he didn't have that kind of money. So he "borrowed" money from PMC.

That money didn't belong to Property Mortgage, of course. It belonged to the people who had invested it with the company.

Embezzling almost always starts out with somebody saying, "I can just take a little bit of this money, and then I'll put it back." It never gets better; it just gets worse.

Perhaps a bookkeeper at a small company realizes it's easy to write a check for a fictitious invoice, and he steals $100, or $500. Then he does it again, and again. Eventually he has stolen $50,000 or $100,000. Once he starts, it's so hard to stop and so easy to continue, especially as time goes on and nobody notices.

The only difference with a senior executive is that the amounts can be bigger. He may take, say, $1 million to invest in what he thinks is a great deal, one that will double "his" money. A year from now, he tells himself, he'll cash out for $2 million, put the money back, and keep the extra million for himself.

Except, of course, the "sure thing" doesn't pay off. So he decides to take more money, to hold onto the investment he made and put more cash into another deal he is sure will turn a big enough profit to pay back what he's taken.

The amounts he has stolen keep growing, year after year, until he is caught.

Often one of my limited partners who has invested in several properties will notice that each of my partnerships has its own bank account, and will ask why I don't just use one account for all of them. I explain that I want everything kept separate, so it's easy to make sure nothing gets mixed up and no money gets lost. Am I suspicious? No, I'm human, and I know how easy it is to feel tempted.

There were times when things were very tight and I wasn't sure I'd have enough income to cover everything. I'd think, gee, there's all this money sitting in this account and that account... But it's not my money. I'm just overseeing it. I didn't ever come close to taking it, because I just couldn't do it.

For me, it's just better to tell the bank or a creditor that I can't pay them right now. I may be embarrassed, but that's nothing compared to how bad I would feel if I took someone else's money – money that had been entrusted to me.

As I had anticipated when I first learned about the meltdown at Property Mortgage, federal regulators descended on Sherman Oaks S&L like a hurricane.

I know real estate, and was confident in my ability to run NSB and our real estate investments. But I didn't run the S&L, and I didn't really know what the regulators would uncover.

Initially, the investigators told our board, including me, "We think that you could be liable for criminal negligence."

Fortunately, that didn't happen. Because so many people at the bank were involved in reviewing and approving loans, Stan couldn't do at the S&L what he did at his own company.

We also had a very thorough annual review by an outside auditing firm, which would have caught any suspicious activity.

The federal regulators did require us to increase our capital, so we investors had to put in some more money – I think I had to add $70,000 to the $500,000 I had originally invested. Once that was done, the regulators gave us a clean bill of health. With things back to normal, I resigned.

The whole experience was very difficult for me, and I realized that, when there's a lot of money around and I'm not going to be watching it myself, I should not be involved.

The S&L industry boomed in the early 1980s. Many began to pay higher and higher rates to depositors to attract funds, and some invested in riskier and riskier projects, hoping to earn big returns.

The bubble began to deflate in 1988. Federal regulators seized some S&Ls, others failed, and Congress set up the Resolution Trust Corporation, which shuttered nearly 750 S&Ls over the next several years, including ours.

Our depositors and borrowers were fine, but as an investor I lost almost $600,000, and I figure I was lucky. I was delighted to be finished with the S&L business. After too many nights with bad dreams, I was sleeping well again.

Whenever I make an investment outside of real estate, I never invest more than I'm willing to lose. It's not money I need for my business to run. If the investment goes bad, that's a shame, but it's not going to ruin me, or hurt my wife and children. And fortunately, some other investments have done very well.

I've enjoyed a very different kind of return in what I regard as the most important investments I've ever made: giving money away. More correctly, giving back.

The satisfaction I've received is greater than anything I'd get from some material possession. I have friends, some with far more wealth than I have, who can't seem to get to the point of saying to themselves, "What am I doing with all this? I'll never use it. Why don't I give more of it away?"

I tell them to look at students at places like the Field Center for Entrepreneurship at Baruch College's Zicklin School of Business, who are just like we were all those years ago. "They are you. Why don't you donate the money that can give them the chance to live the American dream, like we have?"

I remind them that, when they are gone, their heirs will decide what to do with their money. Wouldn't they prefer to decide now where it will go? But some are just not ready yet.

A Taste of the Coffee Business

My support for Baruch College reflects the special attachment I feel to the school. A large part of that is because my connection with Ketchum '52 — my group of close friends from college — has touched almost every phase of my life.

For example, I got into the coffee business with Planet Java because of two men from Ketchum '52, Mort Weinstein and Herb Dallis.

The Dallis Coffee Company was started in Queens by Herb's father and uncle, in about 1915. Every once in a while Herb would take a bunch of us Ketchum guys to visit the company, because he wanted to show us how they roasted coffee.

Herb took over the business from his father and uncle. Eventually his son, David Dallis, came aboard, and by the middle of the 1990s David was running the company.

Mort Weinstein married, had two children, divorced, and then married a physician who was born in Italy and had gone to medical school there. Mort was a very good administrator.

He helped her start a practice in holistic medicine. It was a big fad, and very lucrative. People would go in for three hours, and get their blood pumped out and back in again, at $100 per treatment. Mort said 15 or 20 people would be lying on couches, having their blood moved around.

In 1996, after they had been married for 18 years, his wife said she wanted a divorce. Mort said he thought the practice was worth at least $5 million, and proposed a fair settlement.

Since she was an MD and the business was a medical practice, everything was in her name. She said it was her business, that under New York law she didn't have to pay him anything, and that was that.

So Mort had no job, and no place to live.

Herb asked Mort to come to work for Dallis Coffee, because they needed a good administrator. It was known as one of the best coffee roasters in New York, and very profitable.

It was a *mitzvah* for Herb to bring Mort in, because it gave him a fresh start and a productive position while he and his wife battled over the divorce, which went on for five years.

As a brilliant administrator, Mort transformed the Dallis Coffee Company. He modernized their procedures and systems, and encouraged them to look at opportunities beyond their core business of roasting coffee and selling it to the biggest and finest restaurants in New York City, who were their major customers.

Mort met and became friendly with one of their customers, a guy in his early thirties named Larry Trachtenbroit, who sold coffee to 500 or so Subway sandwich stores in Canada.

Larry told Mort he had an idea for a bottled coffee product that could compete with Starbucks' Frappuccino.

Mort relayed the idea to Herb, who pooh-poohed the idea. But his son David was interested, and he and Mort decided to form a company with Larry to produce it.

Larry was brought up in the Hamptons, on Long Island. It's a wealthy area, but he came from a family of modest means. His father had a video store. When Larry was 21, he started a one-hour photo place behind his father's store, and served coffee to customers who wanted to wait while their film was processed. His father sold the video business and opened up a chicken franchise, but died about six months later.

Larry took over the store, then realized he couldn't compete with Kentucky Fried Chicken, so he opened a Subway sandwich shop. He had a lot of extra space in his store, so he decided to put a Taco Bell in part the store. The Subway people objected, thinking they would lose sales, but Larry insisted, and sure enough, sandwich sales increased. With more choices available, more customers came in.

After a couple of years, he told Subway he didn't think the coffee they supplied was very good, and wanted to use Dallis Brothers coffee. Subway didn't care, because they got a percentage of total sales.

He tried to get other Subway stores in his area to try the coffee, but they didn't want to pay the higher cost. He then reached out to Subway franchisees in the eastern part of Canada, and over time signed up hundreds of them as customers.

Larry liked coffee as a business more than as a drink. He saw an opportunity to compete with Frappuccino with a cold bottled coffee drink, which he planned to call Planet Java.

Mort asked Larry to prepare a number of flavors and blends for taste tests by Dallis Brothers employees, who really knew coffee. They selected five.

Larry, David, Mort and Dallis Brothers Coffee put up about $200,000 to launch Planet Java, but they quickly realized that wasn't enough. The bottling companies that would produce the drink required a deposit of $100,000 just to cover the costs of bottles, labels, equipment changes and so on.

The guys raised another half million from some venture capital investors, and began production.

They soon discovered that it's tough for a small company to get distribution and space on store shelves and in vending machines. Larry decided that, since Pepsi-Cola bottled and distributed Frappuccino for Starbucks, he would try to make a deal with Coca-Cola.

The Coke bottling company in New York is called Coca-Cola Enterprises. It's one of the largest bottlers in the country.

Larry walked into their offices, with no appointment, and asked to see the president. Larry does not look like Central Casting's idea of a corporate executive. He's about five six and weighs about 230. In the summer he wears T-shirts, and in the winter one or two sweatshirts. He had dyed his hair blond, just for fun. The first time I met him it was in February, and he was wearing two sweatshirts, khaki pants, and sneakers.

The Coke receptionist asked if she could tell the president the reason for Larry's visit. "Tell him I have a product that I would like Coca-Cola to bottle and distribute. It competes with Frappuccino, which is distributed and sold by Pepsi." The receptionist went back to the president's office.

And here we see the role that good luck or pure chance can play in business.

First, the president happened to be in, which is fortunate because no middle manager would have bothered to see Trachtenbroit.

Second, the president was keenly aware that Coke USA had been searching for months to find a product to compete with Frappuccino.

It's not that they wanted to take on Starbucks. They were annoyed that Pepsi, their arch competitor, was trying to use Frappuccino to get a foothold in big Coke accounts such as McDonald's and Burger King.

The president met with Larry, who showed him a few bottles. The president decided to run an impromptu test. He had 20 or 30 Coke employees — secretaries, executives, plant workers, drivers— brought into a conference room, and had them taste four flavors of Planet Java.

The results were unanimous. They all liked at least one of the flavors. The president said, "Larry, I think we'd like to work out something with you."

He asked him to fly to Atlanta, to meet the president of Coke USA and Douglas Daft, the chairman and CEO of Coca-Cola worldwide, who came in from Europe.

Daft liked the product, and said to Larry, "We don't want to just bottle and distribute. For Coke to spend $20 million or $30 million in advertising, we have to own the name and the formula."

They worked out a deal that made everybody happy. The venture capital investors got $1 million for their $500,000 investment.

Larry, David, Mort and Dallis Brothers got their $200,000 back plus a small profit, along with a license to market ground coffee under the Planet Java Coffee brand. They figured the huge amount of advertising Coke would be doing for the bottled drink would help them sell their ground coffee.

Larry, the genius behind it all, got a very generous three-year consulting contract from Coke.

I got involved by putting a small amount of money into GLB Coffee Company, which Mort, Larry and Dave formed to produce the Planet Java ground coffee.

Early in 2001 I was in New York, and asked Mort to introduce me to Larry because I wanted to nominate him for Entrepreneur of the Year at the Field Center for Entrepreneurship.

I was having dinner with some Ketchum '52 friends, and invited Larry to join us. He did, and brought along some bottles of Planet Java. He showed up wearing two sweatshirts.

He said the Coke executives treated him so well he was in danger of being spoiled. The press had picked up on his story. He told us that CNN had invited him in for an interview, and when he showed up with a dozen bottles of his coffee, the guard stopped him and said the delivery door was in the back.

Coke had been nervous about what he would say, but Larry raved to the CNN interviewer about how great Coke was as a business partner, and there was a collective sigh of relief in Atlanta.

At the dinner, Mort said they needed to raise about $150,000 to buy coffee beans and hire staff for production of the liquid and ground Planet Java coffee. Larry, Dave and Mort would each put in $25,000, and they'd raise $75,000 from others. "I'll take the seventy-five," I said. Herb heard me from across the table, and said "I'll take 5% of whatever Field takes."

The next day Mort called and said that, after Larry and Dave heard I was willing to put up $75,000, they each decided to invest $5,000 more. I said, "Fine, I'll take the sixty." Well, they had also promised their accountant he could invest $15,000. "Okay, I'll take forty five." No, their insurance man also wanted to put in $15,000. "Then I'll take thirty." In the end, I wound up with about 3% of the Planet Java ground coffee business.

It was fun for me. I got a close-up seat to root for the success of a bright young entrepreneur.

Tranchtenbroit's idea, and the several successful ones he has come up since then, prove to me that there is still hope and opportunity for everybody.

People look back at business pioneers like Carnegie and Rockefeller and talk about what characters those old guys were. Well, here's a real character, and he was a success when he was just 36 years old, which I think is fabulous.

Mom and Dad

Much of this book has focused on my business affairs, but in fact the central element in my life has always been my family. So I would like to include some reflections on my roles as son, husband, father and grandfather.

Resolving my feelings about my mom was a struggle that lasted for many years. To the very end of her life, when she and my dad were living here in Los Angeles, she was a negative, unhappy person, depressed and always anticipating the worst that could happen. Because I have a very positive outlook, I couldn't understand her attitude.

In retrospect, it was foolish of me to allow myself to get so upset by her. There was nothing I could do to change her. Later in life, I was better able to simply accept it – that's who she is, that's what she's going to do and say, and there's no use expecting otherwise. But she still was able to get me upset.

Perhaps I got my personality from my father, because his outlook was very similar to mine. He liked everybody, and always looked for the good side of people.

He opened his grocery store in the midst of the Great Depression, when times were hard for everyone. Often his customers had no money to feed their families until their next paycheck, and he would let them buy on credit. They'd pay him back in a couple of weeks, or a month.

Then, when they had a little cash in their pocket, they'd shop at the supermarkets, where things were a penny or two cheaper.

I told my father I thought his customers were unfair to shop at the chain stores after he had done them such a big favor, but it didn't bother him. He just explained that people have to do what's best for their families.

So yes, I was influenced by my father and his demeanor, always smiling, happy, telling jokes and stories.

I eventually made peace with myself about my mother — not with her, but within myself, because I came to the conclusion that I couldn't change her, but I could control how I felt about her and how I responded to her.

I remember an incident when I was visiting her and she wanted to give some money as Hanukkah gifts to Lisa and Robyn, who were young children at the time.

She took out her checkbook, and sat there. She said, "Let me see now, what did I give last year?" I said, "You gave them fifty dollars each." "Should I do the same thing?" "Yeah, I think you should." "Do I have enough money?" I said, "Mother, you've got more than enough to cover this hundred dollars."

She sat there, holding the pen, thinking about it. "I haven't seen the balance in a long time." "Mother, you haven't seen the balance in years, you don't look at the balance anymore. Don't worry, the money is there. It's okay."

It took her 20 minutes to write the checks.

Years before, I would have been upset, told her to come on, sign it, what are you waiting for – browbeating her. But before I went over there, I knew that I'd have to be patient. I was going to be visiting with her for an hour, and it really didn't make any difference whether we spent some of that time taking a walk or with her holding the pen. So why should I force her to sign in ten minutes or five minutes or two minutes? It didn't matter. I was going to be there for an hour.

I think it's good for people to really look at themselves and

192

realize that they can only change themselves. When you understand that, you have a much more peaceful attitude about yourself.

Gene, Rose and I in their Florida apartment

Marriage

Including the six months we were together before we married, Eris and I were a couple for almost half a century. We met by pure happenstance; some friends invited her to join them for a weekend on Fire Island, and a different set of friends made a similar invitation to me.

If either of us had gone on a different weekend, or if the houses we were staying at had been a little further apart, our lives would have been very different. But we did meet on that rainy weekend, and I am so grateful for the years we had together.

Eris in the mid-1970s

We had a real marriage, not something from a storybook or

TV show. There were bumps along the road, we had our fights and some unhappiness, and in the end, after battling diabetes for much of her life, Eris was taken by lung cancer.

Early in our marriage we learned to compromise. It's not a good marriage if one person is always the boss. I know a lot of men who have big egos and feel they must get their way. That never bothered me. I know there are things I am good at, but I also knew it was important for Eris to be in charge in some areas.

Early on we had one joint checking account. She'd write checks and I'd write checks. I was very exact about mine, and Eris sometimes wasn't. That became a big source of contention with us.

A year after we were married, we decided we each would have our own checking account. Both of us could sign on the other's account, but we didn't. I never even looked at her account, because it didn't matter to me. The idea was a godsend. No more squabbles about checks!

Sometimes it's good to say, "It doesn't matter," or "This is the other person's job." I don't particularly enjoy shopping for clothes, so I never buy them. Eris started buying them for me. At first it was kind of a joke, but it became something quite nice, one spouse doing something for the other. Eris enjoyed it, even though she would sometimes kiddingly complain about what a chore it was, and it made me feel cared for.

Whether it's cooking a meal or bringing home a gift or flowers, it's important to do things that make your wife or husband feel loved and cherished. In a marriage, a lot of effort and energy are directed to raising the children. For the spouse who is home with them all day, that can be exhausting. Anything you can do to brighten your spouse's day can make a big difference.

Eris' rule was that I had to take care of Lisa and Robyn on Saturday and Sunday, because from Monday to Friday I was rarely home before late in the evening. That turned out to be a good arrangement, and the girls and I grew closer because of our weekends together. We have great memories of school trips to Yosemite and Idyllwild. I became the father that a lot of kids in their classes got to know.

Eris and I in the mid-1970s

Our doorbell would ring on a Saturday or Sunday, and when Eris opened the door, the neighborhood kids would say, "Can Mr. Field come out and play?" It was really cute.

They would use our pool or play with our girls, and their parents were happy that someone was with them, keeping an eye on them and running all of the activities and games. I loved it.

Sunday night dinner was usually at one of our favorite local restaurants, Porta Via, with the girls, Anthony and the grandchildren.

We shared a love of travel, and we went on wonderful trips every year with friends and the kids. Our first trip to Israel was a great experience and we had a lot of fun, but it also taught me a lesson.

I broke my wrist playing racquetball five days before we left. The broken wrist meant I couldn't use the traveler's checks; there were two signatures on each check that had to match, and my post-break scrawl looked nothing like the original signature. I took the checks back to the bank, and got new ones that Eris signed.

In Israel, I had to ask her to sign a check every time I wanted to buy something, and she couldn't resist teasing me about my purchases. That taught me a lesson. Never again would I be in a position where I couldn't spend my own money. And it made me realize that it was equally important for Eris to be in charge of hers.

She certainly was good at managing money. As time went on and we got more affluent, the amount of money Eris had for household and personal needs grew, and she put some of that aside – enough that she started to invest in second mortgages. She eventually accumulated about half a million dollars, which was pretty impressive.

I never questioned her about anything that had to do with what we considered her domain, which included all of the shopping. If you question such things all the time, even kidding around, you put the other person in a subservient position. Half of the money was hers anyway.

Eris was famous among her friends for holding themed parties. She also liked to do a surprise birthday party for me every five years. I always knew she was going to do something, but somehow she always managed to surprise me. Twice she did that with parties in our house, which really took some doing. Once it went well, the other time not so much. That time, to get rid of me for the day, she sent me out with her cousin, Bob Blair.

Bob and I had a grand time together visiting restaurants and bars, and we eventually staggered home late and a bit drunk. Eris was very angry, but fortunately for me, she was the ultimate hostess, as always, and no one but Bob and I ever knew.

When we were older, and I was able to take more time away from business, I would take Eris to lunch once in a while. Small things like that can be a big help in helping keep a marriage together. You've got to like the person you're with, have respect for them, and do things that show them how you feel.

That doesn't mean you are never going to have a fight, or that you won't have differences of opinion about things and people. Eris and I had very different views on a lot of subjects, but I think we both learned how to be careful with our words.

We had a wonderful marriage, based on love and mutual respect, and losing Eris was devastating. The person I had cherished and relied on and trusted and admired, my best friend for half a century was gone. I had the support of my daughters, Anthony, my grandchildren and close friends, but it was a difficult, painful adjustment.

After a time, friends would occasionally try to set me up on a date. I am sure the women were very nice, but I wasn't ready.

Then, at one of our Saturday breakfasts at Nate 'n' Al's, Rivka Seiden walked in with Barbara Miller Fox Abramoff. Rivka was the widow of Stan Seiden, one of the city's great theatrical impresarios and producers, and president of Nederlander Theaters West Coast operations.

Rivka and I

I'd met Rivka some years earlier, when Barbara and Frank Abramoff got married. There was a mix-up and there wasn't room at the table where she was supposed to be seated, so Eris invited her to join us.

The guys at Nate 'n' Al's all talked about what an attractive woman Rivka was and urged me to invite her out, but I was too shy.

Luckily for me, she came back to the restaurant a couple of weeks later. This time I worked up the courage to ask her out. She said yes, and we have been together since then. She is a very caring, decent human being, and I am fortunate to again have love in my life.

Leaving Money to the Next Generation

One of the issues faced by any parent who achieves financial success is what to leave to their children. It is natural to want to provide for them. But too often I've seen young people who, knowing they will inherit substantial wealth, are "trust fund babies" who lack not only ambition, but even self-confidence. They seem adrift in a luxurious but aimless lifestyle.

Warren Buffett, a man I admire greatly, said 30 years ago that he is leaving his children "enough money so they feel they can do anything, but not so much that they can do nothing." I think Buffett was exactly right.

You want to provide your children with a safety net, so they will always have an income, but not so much that they can just stop making their own way. You want them to be productive people, to have pride in themselves and in their own accomplishments.

I am fortunate in that Eris and I raised two women who are independent, self-reliant individuals, each of whom created a career for herself with her own dedication and hard work. As parents, most of what we provided was encouragement and admiration.

Lisa, a graduate of Brandeis University, built a very successful catering company, then went into real estate, buying, remodeling and reselling homes.

Robyn, who graduated Phi Beta Kappa from Vassar College, studied at the Architectural Association of London and got her Masters of Arts in Architecture from UCLA. She then became an academic, teaching architectural history and theory at UCLA. Nothing I could leave to them could equal their justifiable pride in what they have achieved on their own.

When my daughters were in their twenties, and had started on their own careers, I told them my plan was to donate most of my estate to the organizations I have been supporting, such as Baruch College, The Field Center for Entrepreneurship, Ben-Gurion University of the Negev, the Los Angeles Philharmonic, Cedars-Sinai, and many others. Each of the girls would receive a relatively modest bequest.

The girls, and later my son-in-law Anthony, were fine with that. They have been investors in my real estate projects for many years, and have reinvested that income in additional projects. Robyn and Anthony have raised Ibby and Kate with the same values, and now that they are in their late teens, they are equally supportive of my philanthropy.

So many of my friends have achieved extraordinary success in business, but feel like failures as parents because their children lack direction, are addicted to drugs or alcohol, or have other problems.

The Jung Institute, named for the Swiss psychiatrist Carl Jung, says, "Many wealthy children experience considerable suffering and deprivation due to lack of self-respect." Inherited wealth can buy many things, but not self-respect.

Long ago I realized that my properties are in my name on paper, but really I am just their caretaker for a period of time. My job is to take care of them to the best of my ability. If I do, they will operate well.

That's true of almost everything in life. If you take care of flowers, they'll blossom. If you take care of your marriage, you and your spouse will be happy. If you take care of your children, they will flourish and grow into self-confident adults.

With my girls at the Lawrence N. Field West Gate of the Hollywood Bowl

Courtesy of the Los Angeles Philharmonic Association

A Nation of Immigrants

From the beginning of the twentieth century until World War II, the greatest influx of immigrants to the United States – like my parents – came from Europe through New York. It was the melting pot of the nation. That's really what gave New York an edge over Chicago, Boston, Philadelphia, Atlanta or New Orleans. The young, energetic and ambitious immigrant population made New York the most exciting and vibrant city in the United States.

In more recent decades, California has been the gateway to America for immigrants from Asia, Latin America and the Middle East as well as Europe.

As I write this, about 40 million people live in our state, or about one out of every eight Americans. If California was a nation instead of a state, it would rank as the fifth-largest in the world, behind only the US as a whole, China, Japan and Germany – larger than the United Kingdom, India, France and Brazil, all of which are manufacturing and trading powerhouses.

Los Angeles today is America's melting pot of immigrants.

When they arrive here with very little, often speaking little English, immigrants have a powerful desire to succeed. They know that, in the nation they left, they didn't have a tenth of the opportunities they enjoy here.

We have people who come from all walks of life who are looking to improve their lives and help their children. To do that in a strange land, you have to work very hard – so they do.

When they first arrive, they will take any job, including jobs that better-off Americans won't. They may open a small shop and work 12 to 14 hours a day, with the family helping out, or start a small business. They believe, as I do, that if you work hard and have a goal, chances are you'll be successful.

Young people who are second- and third-generation Americans take for granted that their parents will take care of them, that they'll go to college, get a job, and have a comfortable life.

But the vast majority of young immigrants, and the children of immigrants, don't have that luxury. They know that they have to make their own way, and may even have to help support the family.

That was my story, for the same reason. My parents came here when they were in their twenties. They worked hard all their lives, and had no money to give me. From the time I was 35, I was partially, then fully, supporting them. But that helped make my success. I knew that I had to take care of them. I had no brothers or sisters, so it was up to me.

What is the reason for the state's amazing growth and success? I believe it is that we have welcomed immigrants.

Like me, the children of field hands, factory workers, gardeners and shopkeepers were able to attend UCLA, Stanford and the state's many other colleges and universities, and became engineers, scientists, doctors, accountants, lawyers, business owners and, yes, real estate people.

California immigrants or their children founded 25 of the Fortune 500 companies. They created enterprises like Apple, Google, eBay, Intel, Tesla, Yahoo!, Panda Express, Disney, Qualcomm, Mattel, and a long list of others.

The momentum hasn't slowed; immigrants own more than a third of all businesses in the state, and they start nearly half of all new businesses – except in technology, where they start *more* than half.

In the United States, you can reinvent yourself. That was the reason for founding the Field Center for Entrepreneurship at Baruch College. Many of the students there are immigrants, the children of immigrants, or from lower-income families.

Many of the companies that get help from the Center are also founded by new Americans.

Eris and I with Anthony, Robyn, Lisa and our grandchildren at the Field Center for Entrepreneurship at Baruch College

I felt that the education I got at Baruch— which cost me and my family almost nothing— gave me a start that changed my life and put me on the path to success. If we let today's immigrants enjoy the same freedoms and opportunities our parents and grandparents enjoyed, America will always be strong.

I'm a firm believer in entrepreneurship, in the freedom Americans enjoy to strive to achieve whatever we wish, whether it be in the arts, sciences, business or some other aspect of life.

The free enterprise system, or capitalism, may not be everything that each of us would like it to be, but to my mind it's certainly better than any of the other systems the world has seen through the years under totalitarians, fascists, communists and socialists. It's like what Winston Churchill said about democracy: it's the worst form of government, except for all the others.

I believe that human nature is such that giving a person the freedom to try whatever they want to accomplish will unleash their abilities.

I'd say the majority of people from all walks of life, and in all professions, are very cautious. Once they find a way to earn enough money to have a family and take care of their children, they become increasingly cautious. The risks that accompany being an entrepreneur seem very frightening to them.

I feel that it's important to be vigilant. There is a creeping bureaucracy in the United States that can hamper entrepreneurship. We also have people who oppose world trade, saying it takes advantage of people in poorer countries. But trade creates jobs in these countries, and teaches skills to their workers.

Do some people flaunt or misuse the wealth the free enterprise system has enabled them to earn? Certainly. But without the drive to accumulate wealth, many of the things we have today wouldn't be around.

Radio, television, life-saving medicines, the smartphone in your pocket, the home you live in and the car you drive – they all were made by people who thought they could make a profit by doing so.

Russia has nuclear weapons, but because of Communist control its economy doesn't even rank in the top 10. The 36 million people in Canada out-produce the 144 million in Russia.

A country that allows its people to strive, and possibly fail, is far better off; those people end up inventing things, creating things and making life better for their fellow citizens and for the world.

Character

As I've said before in these pages, I believe it's vitally important for you to keep your word. And you should certainly live up to what you put in writing. I know people who will make a deal for someone to do a job for, say, $50,000, pay them some money to start, and when the work is done, they demand a discount of $10,000 from the balance they still owe. They figure the guy won't sue, because the amount is too small to hire an attorney and go to court.

That's a bad way to operate, not just for people you do business with, but for yourself. When word gets out that you behave this way, good people are going to hesitate to do business with you. And if you have any sense of integrity, it will hurt you inside. You'll have a hard time looking at yourself in the mirror.

Another window into your integrity, I believe, is how you talk to others. I think people recognize when somebody is sincerely interested when they ask a question. If they sense that you truly want to know what they think, people will respond by helping you. If they trust you, they will do what they can to help you.

I usually avoid publicity about myself. Publicity about the company is fine. But I find that if there is an article in the paper about me, the phone doesn't stop ringing. It takes days and days to get rid of the flakes and the hangers-on and people who now want to make a deal with me. It takes a lot of your time.

But there are people who enjoy publicity, who like to have a high profile and be the center of attention. I have friends who are honored twice a year, every year, by organizations that they are not really active in, but to which they write big checks. They like to be the center of attention. I have no problem with them doing that, but it's not for me.

One way or another, it doesn't take you long to find out about people, at least as far as their business reputation. If you ask around among the people in your business community, 90% of the time you'll find out a lot very quickly. Then, if you meet with the person and talk for a little while, you'll probably have an even better sense of that person's character and integrity.

You may not be able to put it into words, but you'll have an instinct. Sometimes we are reluctant to trust our own judgment; usually that's a mistake.

In business and in my personal life, I don't carry anger with me, at all, no matter what. If I was really angry or upset at ten this morning, it will absolutely be gone when I get up tomorrow morning. I won't even think about it again.

It's not that I'm such a kind or forgiving person. It's because it's my best protection for myself. I don't get bogged down carrying all sorts of negative feelings. They don't do anything useful for me. The person who has gotten me angry doesn't even know that I am carrying around all of these emotions. So it's pointless.

Not too long ago I had someone come up to me, very upset. It turned out that I was thinking about partnering on a deal with a guy who had done something wrong to him 15 years ago. Can you imagine carrying around anger for 15 years over some incident the other guy probably doesn't even remember? What a waste!

It's natural to get angry when someone mistreats you, and it's reasonable to decide that you don't want to be their friend or business associate if that's the kind of person they are. But it makes no sense to me to refuse to say hello to that person at a public event, or to turn around and walk away. I know people who do that. In my view, the trouble with holding onto a grudge or seeking revenge is that you're always thinking about it.

When I was just starting in New York, there was a story in the newspaper about a man who raised money for various real estate projects. It turned out he would sell the same interest in a project twice – that is, someone would buy a 1% share of the project, and he would sell another investor the same 1%. (If you remember the Mel Brooks movie *The Producers*, it's the same idea.) I told an attorney friend of mine that I thought it was terrible. He agreed, but added that we didn't know what might have forced the scammer to commit the fraud.

Speaking at a Baruch College event
Photo courtesy of Baruch College

Then he said, "Ask yourself, Larry, if you could take a million dollars, knowing you'd never get caught, would you do it?" I said, "Never." "How about five million?" "Never."

When we got to fifty million, I had to admit, "Gee, I don't know, that's a lot of money." He said, "Okay, it looks like you'd waver at fifty, and probably at a hundred you'd be gone." I don't think I would, but his point was that you never know why somebody does something. It may be for the basest of motives, and he's just a bad person. But you really don't know the reasons.

So why should I spend days and weeks and months preoccupied and irritated by some wrong I suffered, when I don't even know why it happened?

I dislike arrogance and pomposity in other people, and have gone out of my way to make sure I don't sound like that. Having money or being successful in business doesn't mean you should behave like a big shot. There are a lot of other ways to be successful – as a teacher, scientist, author, artist, or basketball player.

It's fine to take pride in what you have accomplished. But you should be humble enough to recognize that there are a lot of people who have accomplished much more, some of them in areas where you would be a bust. Financial success is not that special, and it sure isn't a reason to be arrogant, bossy or pompous. On the occasions (thankfully rare) when I strayed into that behavior, Eris was very quick to pull me back in line.

Confidence

People who have very quick success often lack confidence. They may say to themselves, "Look at how smart I am, I made all this money." But they may feel, correctly, that they were just lucky, that their success was due to happenstance rather than their effort and skill. It certainly happened during several boom periods of Internet and tech company growth.

To some degree, it happened to me in the first few years when I began buying real estate. Buildings increased in value far beyond the normal rate of appreciation, because of trends I and everyone else had not anticipated. Was I smart to buy real estate? Sure. Did I know values would soar the way they did? Of course not.

I did have the confidence of knowing that I understood the real estate business. If a dot-com kid starts a company and quickly sells it for $50 million or some other extraordinary amount, does he trust in his ability to do it again, or will he be too scared to try?

Warren Buffett has confidence in his decision-making, because he's done it time and again, buying and building companies, most of which are in bread-and-butter businesses, not high tech. If they increase in value by 10% a year, he's thrilled. If it's 5%, he's fine with that.

In real estate, I buy and operate bread-and-butter buildings, not landmarks. It's a model I can replicate time after time, knowing that if I and my people do our jobs right, the buildings will make a nice profit and increase in value over time.

I have been afraid about failing, afraid of making a wrong purchasing decision just before the market changes, or of being overextended. There were a few times when I did feel overextended, because we had buildings for which we couldn't find tenants, and we owed a lot of money to the banks. That was when I came to the conclusion that I simply had to stop holding on to that fear.

Fear can be devastating, and it's often about things you can't change. I couldn't snap my fingers and change the real estate market or come up with tenants, so my fear was pointless.

Instead, I looked at the worst-case scenario: I would have to sell some property to pay back the banks, let some people go, and my lifestyle would suffer somewhat. Even if the very worst happened – and it usually doesn't – I could live with the consequences. That realization made the fear stop.

I try not to hold onto fear, or anger, beyond one night. When I go to bed, it is gone. I can't worry about the same thing the next day. I can get rid of anger fairly easily. Fear is harder, because it slips back, but you can put it aside if you think things through.

Heroes, Icons and Personalities I've Known

When people come into my office, they're often amazed by the wall of photos of family and of myself with presidents, politicians, authors, and other famous people. It's hard for me to believe that someone who came from the Bronx could have gotten to meet all these notable people.

One photo is of an author and wonderful man named Chaim Potok, who I met when he began to paint as well as write. He was active in a group on whose board I served. I asked him why, after being so successful as an author, he had taken up painting. He said, "I think people have creativity in them, and we end up just doing the thing we get to know. I feel like I want to stretch myself in another creative form." I liked his paintings, and bought one.

Near it is a painting by Ivan Schwebel of a street scene in the Bronx, with kids playing stickball. Schwebel was born in West Virginia, but grew up in the Bronx. He enlisted in the Army, and at the end of the Korean War he ended up in Japan, where he studied painting. In 1963 he moved to Israel, where he lived in a tiny house on the top of a hill until his death in 2011. I met him when Eris and I were in Israel for a meeting of the Ben-Gurion University of the Negev. He was a wonderful guy, and a real character.

He didn't like to sell his paintings, which made it tough for him to make a living as an artist!

Also on the wall is a cartoon that was in *The New Yorker*, by one of my Baruch buddies, Mort Gerberg, of a partly-completed building in New York. A sign in the cartoon says "40-story skyscraper under construction," and lists the rental agent as "Lawrence Field Assoc."

I have a lot of friends in the real estate business, but not many have made it into a New Yorker cartoon. I did, thanks to my friend Mort.

I met Ronald Reagan when he was governor and I was on his campaign committee. He was one of the most down-to-earth people I've ever known. He spoke simply and directly, but he had a presence.

I didn't see him much when he became president, of course, but I did from time to time when he was in Los Angeles to meet with small groups of donors. He always remembered the names of people who had supported him early in his political career.

The last time I saw him was at a luncheon at the Peninsula Hotel, when his daughter Maureen was running for office. I sat with him and Maureen, and he talked about the time he first met me when he was campaigning for governor. He appreciated people who stayed with him throughout the presidency.

I realize a lot of people criticized Reagan, saying he was not intellectual or capable at crafting policy, or that he depended too much on other people. I think he was smart to get the best people he could find to work with him, so he could evaluate their ideas and decide which to pursue. He had that ability more than many other presidents. I think Harry Truman was also like that.

One of the most interesting political discussions I ever had was with Jesse Unruh. He was elected to the California State Assembly in the 1950s, and became a major force in Democratic politics in the state. He was a close friend of President John F. Kennedy, and helped convince Robert Kennedy to run for president.

He left the Assembly to run for governor against Reagan in 1970, and of course lost. He was then elected State Treasurer, an office almost nobody had ever heard of, and used it to become what the Wall Street Journal called "the most politically powerful public finance officer outside the U.S. Treasury."

He was powerful, but he was not a popular man. I once went to a luncheon for him downtown, and it ended up that he and I were the only people in the room. That's hard for anyone to take, but it's devastating for a politician. We talked about his life in public office.

He said, "In politics, Larry, you're only as strong and powerful as the help that you can give to people. That's why people support you. It has nothing to do with friendship. It has nothing to do with you being better than somebody else, or being altruistic, or wanting to help people. Your supporters feel that they're buying access to you. Once you're out of that position, they don't need you. Politicians don't have close friends, because we don't have time. We are too busy, either in the legislature or talking to people who we want to support us and give us money."

"Listen, even if they did still build them the way they used to, they still wouldn't build them the way they used to."

Mort Gerberg's New Yorker cartoon showed "Lawrence Field Assoc." as the leasing agent of a skyscraper under construction.

© *New Yorker Magazine, used with permission*

It sounded like a lonely way to live.

In the world of real estate, Robert and Larry Tisch were inspirational, and are among my business heroes. Of the two, I got to know Bob more. He was the people person, and Larry was the numbers guy.

They started with a New Jersey resort hotel in 1946, and built it into a chain of hotels in Atlantic City and the Catskills. In 1960 they bought control of Loews Theaters, which at the time was one of the largest chains of movie houses.

They weren't much interested in the movies. What attracted them was the land under the theaters, many of which they tore down to build apartment buildings and hotels.

They continued to diversify. Loews bought Lorillard, the fifth-largest tobacco company in America, in 1968. In 1974 they bought control of CNA Financial, an insurance company that was nearly bankrupt, but which they quickly put on a sound financial footing. They bought the Bulova Watch Company in 1979.

That's an amazing array of companies to oversee, but they did it well. Bob was a brilliant manager, and Larry was excellent at financing. Each one concentrated on the area where he was strongest.

I remember Larry telling me why he didn't have a secretary or a receptionist, both of which most executives had back then. "For me to get to where I've gotten in business, I've had to have my people involved," he said. "If I answer all the important letters, my managers may never know about what was in the letter, and my thinking behind it. When I make them write the letters, they're going to not just know about it, but handle it. That makes them better managers. And it gives me more time to think about where we should be going as a company and what we should be doing."

As for not having someone to screen his calls, he said, "If I'm not taking calls, I tell the switchboard. When I am taking calls, I pick up the phone. You can get rid of a call in two or three seconds if you want." By talking to some of those callers, he said, he got information about problems his subordinates might not have told him about.

At that time, a lot of companies didn't know what to do with their real estate. It was a drag, and they would sell it just to get rid of it. The Tisches knew about real estate, they knew the market, and they had the courage to step up and buy things when other people were hesitant.

Today, buyers often face competition from big companies and REITS, real estate investment trusts. These big outfits have more money than other buyers, but they can take much longer to make a decision. A quick-moving individual who has access to money can usually come out ahead of somebody much bigger.

A REIT, with hundreds of millions to invest, will be seen as a more attractive buyer than someone like me. But for many of the deals we do, REITS can take a longer time to decide than the seller wants to wait.

In addition, REITs are more interested in larger deals, because it costs them the same to do due diligence on a $20 million deal as on a $200 million project. In effect, the bigger deal is ten times more efficient in terms of their time and effort. They certainly can't move as fast as we can. I learned a lot from Bob and Larry Tisch.

At my desk, surrounded by photos of friends and family

I am always interested in how people do deals. Peter Munk is Hungarian and so am I, or at least my parents were, so I became curious about him when a friend of mine, Daniel Zerfas, told me about him.

Zerfas was working with Adnan Khashoggi, the Saudi Arabian billionaire international arms dealer. Khashoggi had partnered with Munk on a real estate deal in Egypt. They had spent $10 million developing the property, which was going to include hotels, offices and entertainment facilities near the Great Pyramid of Giza.

In 1978, Anwar Sadat, the president of Egypt, decided that foreigners should not control a project of this size, and the government seized the property. Sadat assumed that was the end of the matter. Peter Munk thought otherwise.

Munk was born in Budapest in 1927, into a wealthy Jewish family. He was 16 when the Nazis occupied Hungary. His grandfather gave his entire fortune to the Nazis in exchange for seats on a train that carried 1,684 Jews to safety in Switzerland, including 14 members of his family. (Munk's mother, who had divorced his father years before, did not escape from Hungary. She was sent to Auschwitz, survived, but later committed suicide.)

Munk later went from Switzerland to Canada, where he studied engineering, started an electronics company that went bust, then went into real estate. He bought land in Fiji, built a hotel, and turned that into a chain of 54 resorts in Australia and the South Pacific.

Munk had experienced terrible tragedy and great success, and was not intimidated by Sadat.

He sued the government of Egypt. That, not surprisingly, didn't get him very far in Cairo. Then he sued in the International Court of Justice in The Hague. It took four or five years, but he was awarded a judgment for $10 million. But how was he going to collect it from a sovereign nation?

Munk decided to seize the planes of the government-owned airline. One of its jetliners would touch down in London, Paris or some other airport, and officials of these countries, acting on the court's order, would hold it. Passengers couldn't make their flights, and airport officials were angry because the planes were blocking their gates.

Faced with this chaos at airports all over Europe, the Egyptian government relented and paid Munk and Khashoggi the money they were owed.

Munk was a gambler. After facing down Egypt, he started Barrick Gold in Canada. Others laughed at the venture, but he built it into the world's largest gold producer, and the most valuable company in Canada.

In the United States, he built the TrizecHahn real estate company. We did a deal with TrizecHahn on a building in Westwood.

He gave over $300 million to charities, including universities and hospitals in Canada.

Grateful to the country that took him in, Munk said, "I arrived in this place not speaking the language, not knowing a dog... This is a country that does not ask about your origins, it only concerns itself with your destiny." I admire him greatly.

Real Estate Today: The Future Is Very Bright!

Real estate is still the easiest business to go into, at any age, and build a substantial equity. For me, of course, it was a fabulous journey. There are risks in real estate, as in any business, but I think it is good to take calculated risks. It challenges you, and makes life much more interesting.

Sometimes it can get a little too "interesting," such as when your bank says it wants repayment of that million dollars you've personally guaranteed – and wants it now. That can be frightening. But through it all, I always had confidence in myself.

I was a straight-shooter. I didn't cut corners, or cheat. When you have a reputation as an honest, trustworthy businessman, that's the most valuable asset you can possess.

In the beginning, you may have few assets to invest, or none. To get started, you will have to raise money from other people for your project, and get financing from a bank, insurance company or other source. Once you get going and are operating your properties well, your level of risk actually goes down.

Let's say you build up a real estate portfolio worth $10 million, with $8 million of that borrowed from the bank. Now, something goes wrong – the market turns, or you can't find a new tenant for some space that is being vacated.

If you have to, you can probably sell that $10 million property for $9 million, leaving you with $1 million. That's not good, but it's a lot better than taking a $20,000 loss when you are first starting out and have only $10,000 to your name!

As an entrepreneur, you have to have strengths in different areas: administration, management, negotiation, planning, setting goals, finance, and much more. Aim high; it motivates you and the people around you. Be sure you get good people to help you. Real estate requires a team. You can't do everything yourself. When you find a good person, do everything you can to keep him or her on your team.

Many cities today make it difficult to build new commercial properties. Early on, that can seem beneficial for existing properties, but later it becomes a real cause of concern. Restrictions on development initially make the properties you buy or already own very attractive, because your competitors find it more difficult to build in that city. But over time, the restrictions create a shortage of space for new businesses, or for businesses that want to expand.

I have buildings in areas where it is almost impossible to do new development. If companies grow and need expansion room, and can't find it in Los Angeles, they are going to go to other parts of Southern California, or even locate some of their operations in other parts of the country.

I may lose a tenant who can't find the additional space he needs. Entrepreneurs forming new businesses they expect to grow quickly may decide to start somewhere other than Los Angeles, so they will be able to find the space they anticipate needing.

A real estate investor should look at a property from the viewpoint of a tenant.

If it is an industrial building, will tenants be able to get the water, electricity, natural gas and waste removal services their operations require, at a reasonable price and with the reliability they need? What about road access, for their workers and for trucks delivering raw materials and carrying away finished goods? Does the neighborhood feel safe, so employees will be comfortable going to and fro, even after hours?

Anyone wanting to start in real estate should look at areas that are growing. There certainly are challenges to doing business in California. But it has an amazingly healthy economy, a diversity of industries from high-tech to healthcare to agriculture and much more, and the population continues to grow.

Places like Wyoming or New Mexico, by contrast, may be lovely places to live, but their real estate markets are quite sleepy compared to ours. If you built 2,000 apartments in one of those states, that would probably satisfy the demand for several years. In California, they'd be rented before you painted the front doors.

I am partial to commercial and industrial property, but for someone new to real estate, homes and apartment buildings are probably the safest investment.

If you have a 20-unit apartment building and one tenant moves out, your income drops by only 5%, and you will probably have a new tenant in less than a month.

But let's say you have a commercial property with two tenants that each occupy 50,000 square feet in a 100,000 square foot office space. If one moves out, you suddenly have a 50% decrease in your income, and it can take many months to find a new tenant for all that space.

Because apartments are the most conservative real estate investment, banks will lend you 75% or more of the purchase price. Financing for office buildings, store, warehouses and industrial buildings is generally less generous, requiring you to come up with a larger portion of the purchase price. That of course is a challenge for someone starting out in real estate. But it also means you have less leverage working for you.

If you don't have money, draw up a list of people you know or can get introduced to, and ask them to be limited partners. Gain some experience in the skills you will need: negotiating to purchase property, learning what to look for, how to manage it, and so on. You'll make some mistakes, but you will learn from them and won't make the same ones the next time you buy.

If you start with apartments, you may want to expand into

retail or small offices later, but be cautious.

Key to your success is earning a reasonable return for your partners. If your partners lose on the first deal, they won't be around for the next one.

It's also important to build good relationships with your bankers or other sources of financing. I've worked with a number of banks over the years, but my longest and closest relationship has been with City National Bank, through Damian Doss and Mike Zells, my bankers, and especially with Bram Goldsmith, the Chairman and CEO of City National, and his son Russell, who succeeded him.

The bank financed a lot of my projects, and really helped me – to the point where I was eventually able to return the favor.

Over time I became a big hitter at the bank, with well over a million in balances. Bram had been a real estate developer before joining the bank, so he was interested in what I did.

Then, in the early 1980s, there was a serious recession. A rumor started that City National Bank was shaky. It was untrue, but people got nervous and began to pull money out of the bank – a million a day was going out the door.

Bram invited some of the bank's larger customers, including me to a meeting. We all sat around a big table. He turned to the guy on his left and asked, "How can the bank help you?" Everyone around the table talked about how the bank could help their business.

I was the last one. When it got to me, I said, "Bram, you've asked the wrong question. After all these years of the bank loaning us money so we could prosper, now that we are very secure financially, now is the time for us to help the bank. We have to show the public that people are putting money in – big money. Making the bank stronger is good for us too, because you can lend us more money in the future." The other guys in the room agreed.

I said I'd buy a certificate of deposit – which is the cheapest money a bank gets – for a couple of million, and leave it in the bank. Stanley Black did the same. When word got out that he and I and others were putting money into the bank, the rumors stopped.

A little later one of the guys who worked at City National

asked me what the hell had happened at the meeting. He said, "It's all over the bank that Bram told people, whatever Larry wants to borrow, lend it."

My Philosophy of Money

Money really doesn't matter as much as most people think it does. If somebody has more toys than somebody else, what does it mean? The best thing you can do in life is to find some happiness and have a loving relationship with your family and friends. See your children grow. That's the best thing you can ask or hope for.

I don't think you should be a spendthrift or waste your money, but I think life is to be lived. Whatever you put into life comes back to you. It came back to me as far as charities and mentoring other people are concerned. I get satisfaction out of it. I like to do that. I like to feel that I've helped somebody along the way. I don't look for recognition. It's enough that I know. It makes me feel good.

Most people just need encouragement to go forward. Too often when they ask for advice, the responses they get discourage their dreams or dismiss their ideas. My attitude is different. I believe you should try, so that later in life you don't look back and say, "I should have done that."

The amount of money most people think will bring them

happiness is far greater than what they really need. Financial wealth is a one-dimensional goal, and you need to have many dimensions in life. You should take vacations, spend time with your kids, help others. I was rarely home in the evening during the week when my children were young. But Friday night through Sunday was my time with the kids. The experiences my children and I shared are priceless and irreplaceable.

Remember to take time off – at least a week or two – and go away. If you stay home, your problems will preoccupy you. And when you go away, don't call your office. If the situation is bad enough, they will find you.

It wasn't an easy lesson for me to learn. When we had been married about 20 years, Eris insisted that I tell the people in my office not to call me when we were on vacation unless it was absolutely necessary. Her advice worked. I soon found out how replaceable I was. In fact, in some ways the office ran better without me there. My people knew what to do, so they did it.

When I returned from my first trip, they told me what had transpired, and I praised them for their decisions. I decided to let them make similar decisions even when I was around. Previously, they had fallen into the trap of saying, "Let's ask Larry about it." While I was away, they had to think for themselves. My job got easier, and we were all more successful. And of course my wife and children were much happier to have me with them, rather than watching me disappear every hour to find a phone.

Today so many people – technology people, venture investors, hedge fund operators and so on — have become billionaires. Most people in the world will never possess a tiny fraction of what these people have. Why not use that money, and their skills, for something other than more toys? Show people how to get a decent job or start their own business so they can live well, their children can grow, and they can have a full, varied life.

That's better than having five houses and your own jet. Those things don't bring happiness. And if you measure yourself by what you own, there's always someone who owns more. It's far better to measure yourself by who you are, what you've accomplished that doesn't have a dollar sign attached to it, by who you've helped, how you are respected by your associates, liked by your friends, and loved by your family.

To me, a big part of success is having children who are independent. There are so many people who are crippled emotionally and can't function because they were ignored by their parents. Early on, the mother plays a more pivotal role, but as boys and girls grow older, it becomes terribly important to spend time with their father.

I can see it in the children of people I've met who are crippled emotionally because their fathers never bothered with them. Simply giving money to kids doesn't fix anything. Your children don't want money. They want you to spend time with them.

Talking to students at the Field Center for Entrepreneurship
Photo courtesy of Baruch College

I don't want to buy things. As a matter of fact, I want less stuff. Many people don't realize that having a lot of things is a burden. Let's say you are really rich, and have four houses, a jet and a yacht. Now you have people working for you – a chauffeur, a staff of housekeepers, a yacht captain and crew, a pilot and copilot, and maybe somebody to manage them all.

When you have people working for you, they become your

responsibility, and if they've been with you 10 or 12 years, they're like part of your family. What if you decide you don't want to do this anymore? Do you fire someone who has been a loyal, long-time employee?

As a Jew from a lower-income family, I am a liberal on social issues, like a lot of my friends. But unlike many of them, I am a fiscal conservative. I am fine with giving people welfare when they need help, but we should not take away the drive to get ahead and support yourself.

A lot of "liberals" I know — I don't think the term is even correct— favor policies that end up creating an underclass that is dependent on the government, so we have legions of social workers and community workers. I want us as a society and as individuals to take care of people who are in need, but I want us to create opportunities for them so eventually they can take care of themselves.

How I Do Business

In a negotiation, whenever I let my ego take over and think I'm smarter, better, richer, or right — especially when I am sure I'm right — invariably I lose. I can think of at least half a dozen times when I've been absolutely unwilling to give something up, and it's ended up costing me far more than I could have gained.

These were usually tenant matters, where I thought the tenant had done something in contravention of the lease. Then my ego got involved, so I really pressed. Let's say the tenant is using space outside the building that the lease – as I read it – says he shouldn't. I ask him to stop, he says no, I tell him I'm going to increase the rent and put in cameras, then his lawyers and my lawyers get involved – and then my lawyers say the lease is not so clear, and it's possible we could lose.

So it goes from a situation where maybe I could have collected a few bucks more in rent for the use of the outside space, or maybe not, to where I'm looking at thousands in legal fees, not to mention the time of my people, who have lots of other, more important things to do.

You learn a lot in life, but ego is often the biggest obstacle for us to get over. When you think you are infallible, you're going to take a fall. Even knowing it, I still fall into that trap.

In the real estate business, you have to get comfortable signing notes that obligate you to repay a lot of money. Many people can't bring themselves to do that.

Actually, when I first started out, it didn't really bother me because I knew I wasn't worth that much money. I couldn't pay it back unless the project was successful. Oddly, when you don't have a lot, it's easier to sign notes.

Today I'm more careful, because of course I have the means to pay the money back even if the project fails. Not that I ever failed to pay anything back, but you always have to think about that.

I was able to sleep at night even about projects on which I borrowed heavily, because I always looked at the worst-case scenario before I moved ahead. If I signed a note for $10 million, my analysis showed me that, at the worst, I could lose $200,000 to $500,000, and I could survive that.

It's the nature of real estate that you can pretty accurately calculate your income and expenses. Your property is likely to go up in value over time, but it is very unusual for well-located property to drop significantly.

That's different from other investments, such as the stock market. You can pay $10 a share for a million shares, and lose half of it in a day. Bonds go up and down in value as interest rates change. You can't control that.

But you do control your building. You can change or refurbish the building to make it more attractive to tenants, or reduce the rents slightly, or advertise it more. If you know how to operate real estate and you don't overpay, in the long run you'll do very well.

In the locations we chose to operate in – no more than about an hour's drive from our Beverly Hills offices – real estate values have soared. Some properties have gone up 20-fold.

One example is our Taft shopping center in Woodland Hills. It's appreciated enormously in value, and we could sell it almost instantly if we wanted to. But we can't replace it, because there is no available land in that area.

When I deal with people, whether they are sellers, tenants, consultants, contractors, or my own staff, I treat them the way I would want to be treated. I find it always comes back if you treat people with respect and they have a good feeling toward you.

When I am purchasing a property, I show the seller respect. They may not be real estate professionals – they may own the property through another business, or may have inherited it – but I try to deal with them as if they know as much as I do, and are as smart as I am.

It's also important to treat tenants with regard and consideration, because you want them to behave that way to you. We tell tenants we are very good about fixing everything and keeping the place freshly painted, clean and spotless.

In return, we let them know we are very strict about payment of rent on time. They know the exact amount due every month for the term of the lease, and we let them know it has to be paid on the first of each month, not the tenth or the fifteenth, or even the eighth.

If we have to, we'll impose a penalty, but we generally don't have to do that more than once.

As nice as we are, we are very firm on timely payment of rent. We usually owe money on those buildings, and if we pay the lenders late, they charge us.

I don't enter into negotiations unless I am seriously interested in purchasing a property. Many times people go through the motions, just to see what somebody would settle for, even though they really have no intention of buying. This is a terrible waste of everybody's time. Or they will open up escrow, and then try to negotiate to reduce the price.

I find it is better to check everything very carefully beforehand. Unless it is an extraordinary bargain where I have to move quickly, I use a great deal of care looking into the purchase, and bring in consultants to give me their opinions.

When sellers realize that you are putting in a lot of time and effort, they have a greater level of confidence that the sale will go through. For some sellers, such as large corporations, the certainty that the sale will go through can be just as important as the price.

Real estate is not an area where you can have an exact price. You are not buying a jacket in a department store. For commercial and industrial property, price is generally a function of the income the property generates. The place can look like the Taj Mahal, but you are not going to get a Taj Mahal price if it is not making much money.

When you are buying, you also have to look at any deferred maintenance you will have to rectify once you own the property. That's why as a buyer you require a due diligence period of 30 to 45 days, to thoroughly check the state of the building.

Let's say a property generates $100,000 a year after expenses, and you want a 10% return on your investment. That means the building's value is $1 million.

But if I have to spend $100,000 to make needed repairs, I have to reduce my offer to $900,000, because I am going to spend $100,000 for the repair work.

In the majority of cases the seller will understand the logic of this. We may not get the full reduction – $100,000 in our example – but generally we will get most of it.

There are cases where the seller refuses to adjust the price to cover deferred maintenance, or takes a foolish position about some other issue. I thank them, and move on. I've learned not to chase after deals, because the next one will come along, and it will be as good or maybe even better.

I also believe in making good use of the due diligence time. I look not just at the current income of the property, but its future potential. When this tenant's lease is up in a few years, can you get an additional 25% in rent? If so, that of course increases the value of the building.

That's why I avoid property where the tenants have very long leases. If a tenant has a lease for ten years, in essence he almost owns the property.

The other thing a newcomer to the real estate business must understand is leverage.

If you buy a building for $5 million, you may be able to get $4 million in financing, putting up the other $1 million yourself (alone or with partners.) If the cash flow from the building is paying off the mortgage and giving you $100,000 in income, you control a building worth five times the cash you invested.

If the building goes up 10% in value, your asset is now worth half a million more – which is 50% of the money you put in. Using debt to buy an asset with a relatively small down payment is leverage.

For most people, real estate is the safest and best investment. It is a little harder than buying stocks. Stocks are easy to buy and sell. You can do it on the Internet now. You don't have to know very much to buy stocks, but of course when you don't know a lot, you can end up losing a lot.

As in many cities, there are different markets all around Los Angeles. West LA, Santa Monica, Culver City, El Segundo and Inglewood, for example, are each separate markets.

The more knowledge you have of the local market, the more successful you will be. We focus on buying in good neighborhoods, where tenants will be happy to locate their businesses.

We look for buildings we would be proud of owning, or that we can remodel to be attractive. We have done that with a number of former industrial buildings and warehouses that we've converted to modern and attractive creative office space. If the building we are acquiring was not maintained, we fix it up. After all, if an owner does not take care of a building, the tenant is not going to.

I have lost some deals because I was honest and would only tell the truth. That can bother people who are used to other people telling them what they want to hear, or who have no qualms about lying. Yet lies will always catch up to you.

Say someone asks you how old a building is, and you shave a few years off the correct date. Then the subject comes up again, you forget what you said, and you give them a different date. Or they check the public records and realize you've lied.

Once you've lied about one thing, people know they can't trust you, including on big things. It can be almost impossible to rebuild their trust. The best option is to simply tell the truth. It may be awkward or painful, but it's best for you and the person you're dealing with.

I'm also honest with people who ask for help. I don't lend money to individuals. I will give you money if you can't pay your rent. People offer to sign a note saying they owe me

$1,000, with interest. I don't want to collect interest from you, and I don't want to write notes for $1,000. I will give you the money, and you know you owe it to me. There will be nothing in writing.

If you give it back, fine. It will probably go to somebody else. If you don't give it back, don't ever ask again.

You should always investigate the people you are dealing with.

When we ask people to become our investment partner or joint venture partner, we give them a lot of material about ourselves. If we go to investors who don't already know us, we tell them everything about ourselves, and we give them a list of references to call. That's what everybody should do.

If you are going to do serious business with somebody, you should have them give you a list of references. Character references are at least as important as financial references.

In turn, when we do business with other people, we try to know as much as possible about them.

So here are the key points to my philosophy of real estate:

- Treat people well
- Be honest
- Study the deal carefully
- Don't be greedy
- Don't rush in
- Maintain an outstanding reputation
- Enjoy yourself

Maybe that last suggestion is the most important.

Today, I'm still enjoying my profession, working full-time, and at 88 I'm planning the biggest project of my career in Playa Vista with my friend Frank Gehry, who just turned 90. So don't let anyone tell you you're too old or too young or too anything. Just go out, take smart chances, remember that everything good comes to you through doing well by the people around you, and your life will turn out as mine has ... Not So Bad!!!

You're never too old to have fun!

About the NSB team

The success we've enjoyed over the years is due in large part to the people who have been part of our organization, in many cases for decades. This book would not be complete without acknowledging them:

NAME	YEARS OF SERVICE
Sharon Van Holten	1977 – 2015
Linda Henson	1978 – 2015
Lynette Roxas	1986 – present
Ken Ayeroff	1986 – 2005
Glenn Freeman	1988 – present
Connie Humelbaugh	1998 – 2012
Luis Lapidario	1998 – present
Kevin Mansfield	2000 – present
Anthony O'Carroll	2003 – present
Jeremy Weinstein	2006 – present
Jo Topacio	2007 – present
David Henson	2014 – present
Courtney Roxas	2014 – present
Sharon Mendelovitz	2014 – present
Alejandra Amaya	2017 – present